Ovenless
DESSERTS

OVER 100 DELICIOUS NO-BAKE RECIPES FOR THE PERFECT CAKES, ICE CREAMS, CHOCOLATES, PIES, AND MORE

13-Digit ISBN: 978-1604337648
10-Digit ISBN: 1604337648

This book may be ordered by mail from the publisher. Please include $5.99 for postage and handling.
Please support your local bookseller first!

Books published by Cider Mill Press Book Publishers are available at special discounts for bulk purchases in the United States by corporations, institutions, and other organizations. For more information, please contact the publisher.

Cider Mill Press Book Publishers
"Where Good Books Are Ready for Press"
PO Box 454
12 Spring Street
Kennebunkport, Maine 04046
Visit us online! www.cidermillpress.com

Cover design by Cindy Butler
Interior design by Melissa Gerber
Typography: Bushcraft, Fenwick Park JF, Helvetica Rounded, Neutraface 2 Text, Sentinel
All images used under official license from Shutterstock.com

Printed in China
1 2 3 4 5 6 7 8 9 0
First Edition

Ovenless
DESSERTS

OVER 100 DELICIOUS NO-BAKE RECIPES FOR THE PERFECT CAKES, ICE CREAMS, CHOCOLATES, PIES, AND MORE

MAMIE FENNIMORE

CIDER MILL PRESS

BOOK
PUBLISHERS
KENNEBUNKPORT, MAINE

Contents

Introduction

From my adolescence to this day, I've been responsible for bringing at least one dessert to every holiday party. And while I've made my fair share of pies, cakes, and cookies, what I came to realize is that—since the holidays tend to be those times when I am going 100 mph—turning on the oven is the last thing I want to do.

Maybe it's just me—though the lines I encounter at ice cream stands tell me I'm not alone—but most of my favorite desserts are those that don't require any time in the oven. Give me ice cream, ice cream cake, pudding, salted caramels, or grilled fruit, and I'll give you a smile.

Operating under the suspicion that I'm not the only one who feels this way, I've collected my favorite ovenless recipes so that you can keep the kitchen cool while still dazzling your loved ones. These recipes are perfect for when it's too hot to turn on the oven, or for when you have a million things to do and can't afford to stand by the oven monitoring the progress of a cake. No matter what your situation is, no matter what the occasion, know that there are a number of desserts you can whip up and enjoy!

This collection of recipes contains frozen treats, fresh and fruity delights, as well as an assortment of candies. In other words, there is something to please everyone. And, even though I do have a significant sweet tooth, there are times when savory, salty desserts claim my heart. I've included a number of delicious savory treats here, in the hopes that you, too, will come to see that sweets are not the only acceptable conclusion to a meal.

As busy as we all are these days, there is always the temptation to just buy a dessert at the store. My hope is that these simple recipes, and the rich, elegant scents they will fill your home with, make you lean toward your own kitchen when it is your turn to supply dessert. Remember—homemade will always take the cake!

Frozen Desserts

This section was inspired by my love of ice cream cake, and my penchant for sneaking into the kitchen and stealing secret bites from the freezer. I've never been the biggest fan of cake, but making ice cream the main ingredient transforms any cake from an also-ran into one of life's true pleasures.

There's just something impressive about a frozen homemade dessert—be sure to keep an eye on your family and friends when you serve them these delicious treats, because the joy on their faces is certain to be satisfying. Ice cream, sorbets, and sherbets are also a great way to use up any odds and ends that have been hanging around the kitchen. Don't be afraid to let your creativity run wild—you can toss nuts, fruit, chocolate chips, or candies into almost any of these dishes and still dazzle those who come past your table.

Vanilla Ice Cream

This classic is a true crowd-pleaser. Get some cones and sprinkles ready for your next BBQ—or serve alongside your holiday pies!

1 In a medium saucepan, warm the cream, milk, sugar, and salt over medium heat. As this is warming, beat the five egg yolks in a separate bowl.

2 Once the sugar has dissolved, take approximately one cup from the mixture in the saucepan and whisk it into the bowl containing the egg yolks in order to temper them. Then, add the tempered eggs to the mixture in the saucepan and continue cooking over medium heat until the contents have thickened to where they will coat the back of a spoon.

3 Add the vanilla extract and remove from heat. To ensure that there are no lumps, pour mixture through a fine sieve into a nonstick bowl. Stir the contents of the bowl often as you allow it to cool.

4 When the mixture has cooled, cover with plastic wrap and place it in refrigerator for a minimum of 3-4 hours.

5 Remove from refrigerator and pour chilled mixture into prepared ice cream machine. Churn until it has the consistency of soft-serve ice cream. If you wish, you can also add fruit, chocolate chips, or peanut butter cups at this point.

6 Pour churned cream into container and freeze for a minimum of one hour before serving.

INGREDIENTS

3 cups heavy whipping cream

1 cup whole milk

¾ cup sugar

1 tablespoon pure vanilla extract

1 teaspoon sea salt

5 large egg yolks

Chocolate Ice Cream

MAKES 8 SERVINGS • **ACTIVE TIME: 45 MINUTES**
TOTAL TIME: 5 HOURS AND 45 MINUTES

As we all know, chocolate ice cream is the solution to all of life's problems. Try making it at home—you may not need to buy ice cream ever again.

1 In a medium saucepan, warm the cream, milk, sugar, cocoa powder, espresso powder, and salt over medium heat. As this is warming, beat the five egg yolks in a separate bowl.

2 Once the sugar has dissolved, take approximately one cup from the mixture in the saucepan and whisk it into the bowl containing the egg yolks in order to temper them. Then, add the tempered eggs to the mixture in the saucepan and continue cooking over medium heat until the contents have thickened to where they will coat the back of a spoon.

3 Add the vanilla extract and remove from heat. To ensure there are no lumps, pour mixture through a fine sieve into a nonstick bowl. Stir the contents of the bowl often as you allow it to cool.

4 When the mixture has cooled, cover with plastic wrap and place it in refrigerator for a minimum of 3-4 hours.

5 Remove from refrigerator and pour chilled mixture into prepared ice cream machine. Churn until it has the consistency of soft-serve ice cream. If you wish, you can also add fruit, chocolate chips, or your favorite candy at this point.

6 Pour churned cream into a container and freeze for a minimum of one hour before serving.

INGREDIENTS

3 cups heavy whipping cream

1 cup whole milk

¾ cup sugar

½ cup unsweetened cocoa powder

1 teaspoon instant espresso powder

1 tablespoon pure vanilla extract

1 teaspoon sea salt

5 large egg yolks

Eggless Ice Cream

No eggs, so no need to cook!

INGREDIENTS

3 cups heavy
whipping cream

1 cup whole milk

¾ cup sugar

1 tablespoon pure
vanilla extract

1 teaspoon sea salt

1 Whisk the cream, milk, sugar, vanilla extract, and salt in a bowl until the sugar dissolves (this may take several minutes).

2 Cover bowl with plastic wrap and place in refrigerator for a minimum of 3-4 hours.

3 Remove from refrigerator and pour chilled mixture into prepared ice cream machine. Churn until it has the consistency of soft-serve ice cream. If you wish, you can also add fruit, chocolate chips or your favorite candy at this point.

4 Pour churned cream into a container and freeze for a minimum of one hour before serving.

Variation: For a chocolaty version, add ½ cup of unsweetened cocoa powder.

Strawberry and Lemon Thyme with Goat Milk Ice Cream

MAKES 8 SERVINGS • ACTIVE TIME: 45 MINUTES
TOTAL TIME: 5 HOURS AND 45 MINUTES

I know goat milk may sound odd. But this ice cream is absolutely amazing. One of my favorites!

INGREDIENTS

4 cups goat milk

1 cup sugar

1 tablespoon pure vanilla extract

1 teaspoon sea salt

4 large egg yolks

5 sprigs of fresh lemon thyme

1 pint fresh strawberries

1 In a medium saucepan, warm the goat milk, sugar, salt, and lemon thyme over medium heat. As this is warming, beat the egg yolks in a separate bowl.

2 Once the sugar has dissolved, take approximately one cup from the mixture in the saucepan and whisk it into the bowl containing the egg yolks in order to temper them. Then, add the tempered eggs to the mixture in the saucepan and remove the sprigs of lemon thyme (it's fine if a few leaves remain). Continue cooking over medium heat until the contents have thickened to where they will coat the back of a spoon.

3 Add the vanilla and remove from heat. To ensure there are no lumps, pour mixture through a fine sieve into a nonstick bowl. Stir the contents of the bowl often as you allow it to cool.

4 When the mixture has cooled, cover with plastic wrap and place it in refrigerator for a minimum of 3-4 hours.

5 Remove from refrigerator and pour chilled mixture into prepared ice cream machine. Churn until it has the consistency of soft-serve ice cream. Add chopped strawberries to the cream and churn for another minute or two.

6 Pour churned cream into container and freeze for a minimum of one hour before serving.

Coconut Milk Ice Cream

MAKES 8 SERVINGS • ACTIVE TIME: 45 MINUTES
TOTAL TIME: 5 HOURS AND 45 MINUTES

This ice cream is dairy-free. And it's easy to make it vegan as well—just use agave nectar or cane sugar instead of honey!

INGREDIENTS

2 16-oz. cans of coconut milk

¾ cup honey

3 teaspoons pure vanilla extract

1 teaspoon sea salt

2 tablespoons cornstarch

1 Add ¼ cup of the coconut milk and the cornstarch to a bowl and whisk until the cornstarch is dissolved. In a medium saucepan, warm the remaining coconut milk, honey, and sea salt over medium heat. When contents of saucepan are warm, add corn-starch mixture and stir constantly until the contents have thickened to where they will coat the back of a spoon (approximately 6-8 minutes).

2 Remove from heat, pour into bowl and allow to cool.

3 When the mixture has cooled, cover with plastic wrap and place it in refrigerator for a minimum of 3-4 hours.

4 Remove from refrigerator and pour chilled mixture into prepared ice cream machine. Churn until it has the consistency of soft-serve ice cream.

5 Pour churned cream into container and freeze for a minimum of one hour before serving.

Strawberry Sorbet

MAKES 8 SERVINGS • ACTIVE TIME: 25 MINUTES
TOTAL TIME: 5 HOURS AND 25 MINUTES

Take advantage of sweet summer strawberries by incorporating them in this chilled dessert.

INGREDIENTS

1 cup sugar

½ cup water

½ teaspoon sea salt

3 pints fresh strawberries

¼ cup freshly squeezed lemon juice

1 teaspoon lemon zest

1 Heat sugar and water in a medium saucepan until sugar is dissolved completely. Let cool.

2 Remove stems from strawberries. Place into food processor with lemon juice and lemon zest, and blend until smooth. Add the cooled syrup and blend until thoroughly mixed.

3 Place mixture into refrigerator and chill for 2-3 hours.

4 Remove from refrigerator and pour into ice cream maker. If you are not a fan of seeds, run the mixture through a fine mesh sieve before pouring into ice cream maker. Churn sorbet for approximately 20 minutes, until it is the consistency of soft-serve ice cream.

5 Pour churned sorbet into container and freeze for a minimum of one hour before serving.

Variation: Use blueberries, pineapple, mango, raspberries, etc. Any fresh fruit will work!

Variation: Steep your favorite herb in the simple syrup: mint, thyme, basil, cilantro, lavender, etc.

Orange Sherbet

The difference between sorbet and sherbet? Sherbets contain milk, whereas sorbets do not. Milk or no, both are delicious!

INGREDIENTS

⅓ cup sugar

3 cups freshly squeezed orange juice

Zest of 1 orange

½ teaspoon sea salt

2 tablespoons freshly squeezed lemon juice

¼ teaspoon pure vanilla extract

1½ cups whole milk

2 tablespoons Cointreau or Triple Sec

1 Combine all ingredients, with the exception of the liqueur, in a bowl. Mix until sugar is completely dissolved. Chill in the refrigerator for 3-4 hours.

2 Remove from refrigerator and pour into ice cream machine. Churn until mixture has the consistency of soft-serve ice cream. Add the liqueur and churn until incorporated.

3 Pour mixture into container and freeze for 1-2 hours before serving.

Watermelon Granita

Wondering what to do with all of that leftover watermelon? Try using it in a granita. I like to serve this as a palate cleanser between courses.

INGREDIENTS

4 cups fresh watermelon pieces

½ cup sugar

2 tablespoons freshly squeezed lime juice

2 tablespoons honey

1 Place all ingredients in a food processor and blend until smooth.

2 Pour mixture into baking dish and place in the freezer for approximately two hours.

3 Remove dish from freezer and scrape top with a fork until the surface is covered with icy flakes. Return to freezer for one hour and repeat the scraping.

4 Serve flakes in tiny bowls as a palate cleanser or a light summer dessert.

Frozen Yogurt

MAKES 6-8 SERVINGS • ACTIVE TIME: 10 MINUTES
TOTAL TIME: 5 HOURS AND 10 MINUTES

Froyo anyone?!?

1 Mix all ingredients in a bowl and let sit long enough for the sugar to dissolve.

2 Place bowl in refrigerator and allow to chill for at least one hour.

3 Remove from refrigerator and pour mixture into ice cream machine. Churn until it has the consistency of soft-serve ice cream.

4 Pour churned yogurt into container and freeze for a minimum of two hours before serving.

INGREDIENTS

3 cups of plain
Greek yogurt

⅓ cup sugar

⅓ cup honey

1 teaspoon
vanilla extract

Italian Ice

MAKES 2 SERVINGS • ACTIVE TIME: 5 MINUTES
TOTAL TIME: 2 HOURS AND 30 MINUTES

Chill out with your friends with a casual and fun dessert like Italian ice.

INGREDIENTS

1 ½ cups water

¾ cup sugar

Juice of ½ lemon

1 teaspoon of your favorite oil or extract (lemon, lime, mango, pineapple, peach, cherry, bubblegum, strawberry, etc.)

1 Add water and sugar to a saucepan and heat over medium-high heat until sugar has dissolved. Add lemon juice and desired flavoring.

2 Turn off heat and allow to cool. Pour mixture into ice cream maker and churn for 20-30 minutes. Transfer to another container and let freeze for at least two hours before serving.

30 Frozen

Lemon-Thyme Ice Lollies

**MAKES 4-6 SERVINGS • ACTIVE TIME: 5 MINUTES
TOTAL TIME: 2 HOURS AND 30 MINUTES**

Lemons and fresh herbs are typically used to brighten the other flavors in a dish. Let them shine in this light and refreshing dessert.

INGREDIENTS

4 cups water

1 cup sugar

2 large bunches of fresh thyme

2 cups freshly squeezed lemon juice

1 teaspoon lemon zest

1 In a saucepan, combine one cup of the water and the sugar, and cook over medium heat until sugar is dissolved. Add the thyme to the pan and let cook for two minutes. Remove pan from heat and allow syrup to cool.

2 When the mixture is cool, remove the thyme.

3 Combine thyme-infused syrup, lemon juice, and three cups of water in a food processor or blender. Blend until thoroughly combined.

4 Pour mixture into popsicle molds, freeze for 30 minutes and remove to insert popsicle sticks. Return to freezer and freeze until solid.

Variation: Prefer a different herb? Use your favorite—or try basil, rosemary, lavender, or mint!

Frozen Pineapple Pops

**MAKES 8-10 SERVINGS • ACTIVE TIME: 5 MINUTES
TOTAL TIME: 4 HOURS AND 35 MINUTES**

Fruity ice pops are refreshing and can cool you down on even the hottest summer day. This is also a great way to use your fresh fruit when it's about to get a little bit too ripe.

INGREDIENTS

3 cups fresh pineapple, chopped

¼ cup sugar

3 tablespoons honey

¼ cup plain Greek yogurt

2 tablespoons freshly squeezed lemon juice

1 Place all ingredients in a blender or food processor and blend until smooth.

2 Pour mixture into popsicle molds and freeze for 30 minutes.

3 Remove from freezer and insert popsicle sticks. Return to freezer and freeze for a minimum of four hours, or until completely frozen.

Variation: Use three cups of any fresh or frozen fruit you have on hand. Blueberries, strawberries, honeydew melon, watermelon, mango, peaches, and blackberries are all wonderful—you can't make a wrong move!

Ice Cream Cake

MAKES 8-10 SERVINGS • ACTIVE TIME: 20 MINUTES
TOTAL TIME: 1 HOUR AND 20 MINUTES

Ice cream cake has been a staple in my life for as long as I can remember. I have a summer birthday, so turning on the oven feels sinful. Plus, I'm not the biggest fan of cake. The solution? Ice cream cake. They are so easy and versatile. And you can easily adjust the recipe to feature whatever flavor you like!

INGREDIENTS

6-8 classic ice cream sandwiches

1 large package of Oreo cookies

¼ cup whole milk

1 large container vanilla ice cream

1 container Cool Whip

1 Place Oreos in a blender or food processor. Process until finely ground.

2 Line the bottom of a springform pan with the ice cream sandwiches. Feel free to break into pieces in order to completely cover the pan's bottom.

3 Mix ½ cup of ground Oreos and the milk. Spread this mixture over the ice cream sandwiches.

4 Alternate layers of ice cream and Oreos until you reach the top of the pan. Reserve approximately ¼ cup of Oreo crumbs.

5 Top with Cool Whip and sprinkle remaining Oreo crumbs on top.

6 Place pan in freezer for a minimum of one hour before serving.

Minty Icebox Pie

MAKES 6-8 SERVINGS • ACTIVE TIME: 25 MINUTES
TOTAL TIME: 4 HOURS AND 25 MINUTES

This cooling treat is minty fresh and is sure to be a hit among family and friends!

1 Place five tablespoons of butter in a frying pan and melt over medium heat. When butter is melted, remove from heat and place butter in bowl with two cups of the thin mints and the sugar. Stir to combine and then press into the bottom of an eight- or nine-inch springform pan.

2 Place cream and powdered sugar in a bowl and whisk until soft peaks form. Set aside, reserving ¹/₂ cup for the top of the pie.

3 Place cream cheese in a separate bowl and beat until light and fluffy. Add mint extract and stir to combine. Fold in mini-chocolate chips and remaining thin mints. Scoop mixture on top of crust, place pan into refrigerator and chill for a minimum of two hours.

4 Place remaining butter, dark chocolate chips, water, and corn syrup in a microwave-safe bowl and microwave until melted, approximately 30-45 seconds. Remove pie from refrigerator and pour chocolate mixture on top. Place pie in freezer for 1-3 hours.

5 When ready to serve, remove pie from freezer and top with reserved whipped cream.

INGREDIENTS

2 ½ cups thin mint cookies, ground (reserve ½ cup for filling)

7 tablespoons butter (2 tablespoons reserved for top layer)

2 tablespoons all-purpose flour

1 tablespoon sugar

1 ½ cup heavy whipping cream

6 tablespoons powdered sugar

8 oz. cream cheese

1 cup Marshmallow Fluff

¼ teaspoon pure mint extract

1 cup mini-chocolate chips

¾ cup dark chocolate chips

2 tablespoons water

3 teaspoons corn syrup

Classic Vanilla Milkshake

MAKES 2 SERVINGS • ACTIVE TIME: 5 MINUTES
TOTAL TIME: 5 MINUTES

The milkshake is a true classic. One of my favorite ways to enjoy ice cream.

Place all ingredients in a blender and blend until combined. Pour into tall glasses and serve with straws!

Variation: For a chocolate milkshake, use the same amount of chocolate ice cream or add one cup of chocolate syrup. If a malted milkshake is your thing, add ½ cup of malted milk powder.

INGREDIENTS

1 pint of vanilla
ice cream

¼ cup
whole milk

¼ teaspoon
sea salt

1 teaspoon
vanilla extract

Ground cinnamon,
as garnish

Roasted Marshmallow Milkshake

Get your guests to make dessert for you! Pay attention to the contrast between the warm toasted flavor of the marshmallow and the cold ice cream.

1 Roast marshmallows to desired color over an open flame. Either a grill or gas stovetop will work.

2 Once marshmallows are roasted, add all ingredients to a blender and blend until combined.

3 Pour into tall glasses and serve.

INGREDIENTS

8 marshmallows

1 pint vanilla ice cream

¼ cup whole milk

¼ teaspoon sea salt

1 teaspoon vanilla extract

Ice Cream Soda

MAKES 1 SERVING • ACTIVE TIME: 5 MINUTES
TOTAL TIME: 5 MINUTES

A great fizzy treat!

INGREDIENTS

3 tablespoons
heavy cream

1 teaspoon
pure vanilla extract

2 scoops
vanilla ice cream

Seltzer water

1 Pour cream and vanilla extract into a tall glass.

2 Slowly stir in the seltzer water until glass is approximately two-thirds full.

3 Add ice cream to glass.

4 Top with seltzer. Garnish with sprig of fresh mint and serve with a straw.

Frozen Chocolate-Covered Bananas

MAKES 1 SERVING • ACTIVE TIME: 5 MINUTES
TOTAL TIME: 5 MINUTES

Bananas are easy to eat, and you can claim these are a healthy dessert. Perfect for kids and adults.

INGREDIENTS

3 bananas, not too ripe

12 oz. semi-sweet chocolate

1 tablespoon butter, softened

¼ cup salted peanuts

¼ cup rainbow sprinkles

¼ cup shredded coconut

1 Cut the bananas into thirds and insert a popsicle stick into each piece. About ⅔ of the stick should be in the banana.

2 Place chocolate in a microwave-safe bowl and microwave for 12-second intervals, removing to stir each time. When the chocolate is almost completely melted, stir in the softened butter. The chocolate should look glossy.

3 Dip bananas in chocolate and spoon chocolate over fruit so that the bananas are completely covered.

4 If desired, roll chocolate-covered banana in topping(s) of your choice.

5 Place covered bananas on a baking sheet lined with wax paper. Place in refrigerator or freezer for 45 minutes to one hour before serving.

Pumpkin Cheesecake Icebox Pie

MAKES 6-8 SERVINGS • ACTIVE TIME: 20 MINUTES
TOTAL TIME: 10 HOURS AND 20 MINUTES

When fall has arrived but summer temperatures are still holding on, try serving this pumpkin delight at one last "summer" BBQ. It works well at Thanksgiving, too!

1 Combine brown sugar, melted butter, and ground gingersnaps in a bowl. Firmly press mixture into the bottom of an eight- or nine-inch springform pan.

2 Place pumpkin and cream cheese into a bowl and beat until light and fluffy. Add allspice, nutmeg, cinnamon, and salt and stir until thoroughly combined. While mixing in the spices and salt, slowly pour the condensed milk into the bowl. Gently fold in Cool Whip.

3 Pour mixture on top of gingersnap crust. Place in freezer, and freeze for a minimum of 10 hours or overnight. When ready to serve, some homemade cinnamon whipped cream makes for a lovely topping.

INGREDIENTS

1 cup canned pumpkin

½ teaspoon ground allspice

½ teaspoon freshly ground nutmeg

1 teaspoon cinnamon

½ teaspoon sea salt

8 oz. cream cheese

1 cup Cool Whip

1 can sweetened condensed milk

2 cups gingersnaps, ground

3 tablespoons dark brown sugar

6 tablespoons butter, melted

S'mores Icebox Cake

MAKES 6-8 SERVINGS • ACTIVE TIME: 20 MINUTES
TOTAL TIME: 5 HOURS AND 20 MINUTES

If you are a s'mores fanatic, try this cold version of the classic!

INGREDIENTS

2 ¾ cups heavy whipping cream

8 oz. Marshmallow Fluff

1½ cup mini-marshmallows

1 bag semi-sweet chocolate chips

1 box graham crackers

1 Place two cups of heavy cream into a bowl and whisk until soft peaks form. Stir in the Fluff, making sure not to deflate the whipped cream. Fold in one cup of the mini-marshmallows.

2 Place the chocolate and remaining cream in a microwave-safe bowl and microwave for 30 seconds. Remove from microwave, let stand for a few seconds, and then stir until smooth. If chocolate is not melted, place back in microwave for 15 seconds.

3 Spread a thin layer of the marshmallow whipped cream on the bottom of a nine-inch baking dish. Place an even layer of graham crackers on top. Place a thick layer of the whipped cream on top of the graham crackers and then add a layer of chocolate. Alternate layers of graham crackers, marshmallow whipped cream, and chocolate until you reach the top of the dish.

4 Top with remaining mini-marshmallows. Pieces of chopped chocolate and graham cracker crumbs also make good toppings. Cover with plastic and refrigerate for five hours, or overnight. When you are ready to serve, you can use a kitchen torch to brown the marshmallows on top. And if you don't, no worries! It's still an amazing treat.

Raspberry Ice Cream Cake

MAKES 8-10 SERVINGS • ACTIVE TIME: 20 MINUTES
TOTAL TIME: 1 HOUR AND 20 MINUTES

Raspberries are tart, sweet, and absolutely perfect in this frozen cake. Serve this instead of strawberry shortcake to shake things up!

1 Line the bottom of a nine-inch springform pan with ladyfingers. Spread a layer of vanilla ice cream on top. Spread a thin layer of raspberry preserves on top of the vanilla ice cream, then add a layer of raspberry ice cream. Add another layer of raspberry preserves on top of the raspberry ice cream. Top with ladyfingers and repeat until you reach the top of the pan.

2 Place into freezer for at least one hour. When ready to serve, whipped cream and fresh raspberries make lovely additions.

INGREDIENTS

1 large package of ladyfingers

1 quart vanilla ice cream

1 quart raspberry ice cream

1 jar of raspberry preserves (seedless if you prefer)

1 pint fresh raspberries

Lemon-Lime Frozen Yogurt

MAKES 4-6 SERVINGS • ACTIVE TIME: 10-20 MINUTES
TOTAL TIME: 2 HOURS AND 20 MINUTES

This yummy froyo is so refreshing, it will cleanse your palate after just one bite. You just might be ready for a second dinner after this one!

INGREDIENTS

2 cups plain Greek yogurt

½ cup water

1 cup simple syrup (1 cup water and 1 cup sugar, heated until sugar is dissolved)

2 tablespoons freshly squeezed lime juice

1 tablespoon freshly squeezed lemon juice

1 teaspoon finely grated lemon zest

1 teaspoon finely grated lime zest

½ teaspoon pure vanilla extract

1 Place all ingredients in a bowl and whisk until well combined. Pour into an ice cream maker and churn until it reaches the consistency of soft-serve ice cream.

2 Pour into an airtight container and freeze for at least two hours. Serve with candied citrus peels as garnish!

Lavender Ice Cream

MAKES 1 QUART • ACTIVE TIME: 20 MINUTES
TOTAL TIME: 8 HOURS

This ice cream is floral and refreshing! I like to top mine with crushed chocolate wafers.

INGREDIENTS

2 cups heavy cream

1 cup half-and-half

⅔ cup honey

2 tablespoons dried lavender

2 large egg yolks

⅛ teaspoon sea salt

1 Place the cream, half-and-half, honey, and lavender in a medium saucepan and cook until it is about to boil. Remove from heat and let stand for at least 30 minutes. When cool, pour the mixture through a fine mesh sieve to remove the lavender.

2 Place the strained mixture in a medium saucepan and cook over medium-low heat. Beat the egg yolks in a separate bowl. Slowly add one cup of the saucepan's contents to the yolks while whisking constantly. Place the egg-and-cream mixture back into the saucepan and cook over medium-low heat while stirring constantly. You want to make sure the cream does not come to a boil.

3 When the mixture is thick enough to coat the back of a wooden spoon, remove the pan from the heat and pour through a fine mesh sieve into a clean bowl. Let cool while stirring a few times during the cooling process. Cover directly with plastic and place into refrigerator for at least four hours.

4 Pour mixture into an ice cream maker and churn until it reaches the consistency of soft-serve ice cream. Transfer to an airtight container and freeze for 2-3 hours before serving.

Chocolate, Peanut Butter, Banana Milkshake

MAKES 2 MILKSHAKES • ACTIVE TIME: 5 MINUTES
TOTAL TIME: 5 MINUTES

Don't forget the sea salt in this recipe. It helps bring out all of the flavors!

Place all ingredients in a blender and blend until well combined. Pour into tall glasses and serve with a straw.

INGREDIENTS

1 pint chocolate ice cream

2 bananas, frozen

½ cup creamy peanut butter

¼ cup whole milk

3 tablespoons chocolate syrup

¼ teaspoon sea salt

Coconut Cream Float

MAKES 1 LARGE OR 2 SMALL SHAKES • ACTIVE TIME: 2 MINUTES
TOTAL TIME: 2 MINUTES

This is the perfect balance between a mudslide and a piña colada!

INGREDIENTS

¾ cup coconut
ice cream

2 cups cream soda

1 tablespoon
chocolate syrup

2 teaspoons
spiced rum

⅛ teaspoon freshly
grated nutmeg

Place the ice cream in the bottom of two glasses. Grate nutmeg over ice cream. Top with equal amounts of cream soda, rum, and the chocolate syrup. Enjoy!

Root Beer Float

MAKES 2 SERVINGS • ACTIVE TIME: 2 MINUTES
TOTAL TIME: 2 MINUTES

This classic is always a great choice for dessert.

Place the ice cream in the bottom of a tall glass. Slowly pour the root beer into the glass and then top with whipped cream.

INGREDIENTS

1 pint vanilla ice cream

2 root beers

Whipped cream for garnish

Coconut Milk Pistachio Ice Cream

MAKES 3 CUPS • ACTIVE TIME: 20 MINUTES
TOTAL TIME: 5 HOURS AND 20 MINUTES

I love pistachio ice cream and thought the coconut milk would add a new dimension. You may even impress yourself with this flavor combination.

INGREDIENTS

1 can coconut milk, full fat

1 cup almond milk

¼ cup honey

½ teaspoon almond extract

2 cups pistachios, shelled and chopped

1 Place the coconut milk, almond milk, honey, almond extract, and half of the pistachios in a blender. Blend on high for three minutes and then place in refrigerator for a minimum of three hours.

2 When the mixture is chilled, pour into prepared ice cream maker and churn until you reach the consistency of soft-serve ice cream. Toss the remaining pistachios toward the end of the churning. Place in an airtight container and freeze for at least two hours. Top with some chocolate shavings or crushed pistachios when serving.

Blueberry-Lemon Granita

MAKES 6-8 SERVINGS • ACTIVE TIME: 10 MINUTES
TOTAL TIME: 4 HOURS AND 10 MINUTES

This granita is a perfect palate cleanser after a meal—or a great way to cool down a summer BBQ!

1 Place all ingredients into a food processor. Blend until well combined and no large pieces remain.

2 Run mixture through a fine mesh sieve and pour liquid into an eight-by-eight-inch baking dish.

3 Place in freezer and scrape with a fork once an hour to loosen tiny, icy flakes.

4 When you have enough flakes, place them into bowls and top with a fresh mint leaf!

INGREDIENTS

1 pint blueberries

1 tablespoon lemon zest

¾ cup freshly squeezed lemon juice

1 cup water

½ cup sugar

1 tablespoon freshly grated ginger root

Frozen Mango Pops

MAKES 10-12 POPSICLES • ACTIVE TIME: 8 MINUTES
TOTAL TIME: 5 HOURS

Here is a delicious vegan option that everyone will love!

INGREDIENTS

3 ripe mangos,
peeled and cubed

2 ½ cups
coconut milk

1 tablespoon freshly
squeezed lemon
juice

1 Place all ingredients in a blender and blend on high until smooth.

2 Pour into popsicle molds and freeze.

3 After 30-45 minutes, insert a popsicle stick into each mold.

4 Freeze for another 4-5 hours or until completely frozen.

Mint Chocolate Chip Milkshake

Top this shake with crushed thin mint cookies for even more mint-and-chocolate flavor.

1 Place all ingredients in a blender and blend until smooth.

2 Pour into tall glasses and serve with a straw.

3 If desired, top with whipped cream!

INGREDIENTS

1 pint mint chocolate chip ice cream

1 cup whole milk

2 tablespoons chocolate syrup

½ cup chocolate chips

Semifreddo with Pistachio and Peach

MAKES 15-20 SLICES • ACTIVE TIME: 20 MINUTES
TOTAL TIME: 5 HOURS AND 20 MINUTES

Semifreddo is cool and creamy. A perfect alternative to ice cream!

INGREDIENTS

8 oz. crème fraîche

½ cup powdered sugar

1 cup heavy whipping cream

½ teaspoon freshly grated nutmeg

¼ cup pistachios, shelled and chopped

Juice of ½ a lime

2 tablespoons honey

¼ cup fresh mint, chopped

3 peaches, sliced

1 Line a loaf pan (roughly eight-by-four) with plastic wrap. The plastic wrap should hang over the pan's edges.

2 Place the crème fraîche and sugar in the bowl of an electric mixer and whisk until soft peaks form. Slowly pour in the heavy cream while the mixer is running. Whisk for approximately three minutes. Fold in the nutmeg and chopped pistachios. Pour mixture into prepared loaf pan, fold plastic over the mixture and freeze for at least five hours.

3 Remove from freezer and let stand for five minutes.

4 While the semifreddo is standing, toss the sliced peaches with the lime juice and honey. Let stand for five minutes.

5 Flip the semifreddo onto a plate. Top with peaches, garnish with the chopped mint, and slice.

Almond-Pignoli Milkshake

MAKES 2 LARGE OR 3 SMALL SHAKES • ACTIVE TIME: 5 MINUTES
TOTAL TIME: 5 MINUTES

Pignoli is the Italian word for pine nut. It also refers to the chewy almond cookies found in many Italian pastry shops. Since this is one of my favorite cookies of all time, I thought: Why not make it into a milkshake?

1 Toast pine nuts in a dry skillet for 30 seconds over high heat, taking care not to burn. Remove pine nuts from pan and let them cool.

2 Place ice cream, almond paste, milk, and salt in a blender and blend until smooth. Pour shake into tall glasses and sprinkle toasted pine nuts on top.

INGREDIENTS

1 pint vanilla ice cream

½ cup almond paste

⅔ cup whole milk

¼ teaspoon sea salt

2 tablespoons pine nuts

Sweet & Savory

A number of people in my life do not have the biggest sweet tooth. When one of them is coming over for dinner, I like to make a savory dessert with just a hint of sweetness. Of course, salt is major player in the savory world, and can enhance just about any sweet treat. A little bit of salt goes along way in a dessert, reducing bitterness and shocking your taste buds awake.

I also bring an extensive background in cheese to the table, and in some cultures this is the classic post-dinner treat. You may hesitate when confronted with blue cheese for dessert, but whipping it with just a hint of honey will convert even the strongest of skeptics, and just may make cheese the official dessert in your house. Pairing cheese with some after-dinner wines (port or Sauternes are personal favorites) will help you see that something sweet isn't the only way to end a meal.

Vanilla Pudding

MAKES 7-8 SERVINGS • ACTIVE TIME: 20 MINUTES
TOTAL TIME: 2 HOURS AND 20 MINUTES

Pudding is incredibly easy to prepare and just about everyone loves it!

INGREDIENTS

⅓ cup sugar

2 cups whole milk

2 tablespoons cornstarch

¼ teaspoon sea salt

2 egg yolks, large

2 tablespoons unsalted butter, softened

2 teaspoons vanilla extract

1 Put egg yolks in a bowl and beat.

2 In a medium saucepan stir the sugar, cornstarch, and salt together. Over medium heat, slowly whisk in the milk and stir constantly until the mixture is smooth. Cook and continue to stir constantly until mixture comes to a boil.

3 Remove saucepan from heat and stir approximately one-third of the mixture into the beaten egg yolks. Stir constantly so that the eggs do not scramble.

4 Pour warmed eggs into saucepan. Cook for one minute, stirring constantly.

5 Remove saucepan from heat. Stir in the vanilla and softened butter.

6 Pour pudding into dessert dishes and place dishes in refrigerator. Allow dishes to chill for a minimum of two hours before serving.

Chocolate Pudding

MAKES 7-8 SERVINGS • **ACTIVE TIME: 20 MINUTES**
TOTAL TIME: 2 HOURS AND 20 MINUTES

I learned how to make chocolate pudding from my grandmother. It is such a fun and rewarding activity for all ages!

1 Add sugar, cocoa powder, cornstarch, and salt to medium saucepan and whisk together. Set over medium heat and slowly pour in the milk while whisking constantly. Cook until mixture thickens and comes to a boil, approximately 8-10 minutes.

2 Reduce heat to low and cook for an additional 1-2 minutes.

3 Remove saucepan from heat. Stir in butter and vanilla.

4 Transfer pudding to serving dishes and cover with plastic wrap, placing wrap directly on the pudding's surface to ensure that a skin does not form. Place in refrigerator and refrigerate for at least two hours. Top with whipped cream and serve!

INGREDIENTS

¼ cup sugar

½ cup sweetened cocoa powder

4 tablespoons cornstarch

2½ cups whole milk

¾ teaspoon sea salt

6 tablespoons butter, softened

2 teaspoons pure vanilla extract

Banana Pudding

MAKES 7-8 SERVINGS • ACTIVE TIME: 15 MINUTES
TOTAL TIME: 6 HOURS AND 20 MINUTES

This Southern classic just got easier! Perfect to serve at the end of a summer BBQ!

INGREDIENTS

3 bananas, not too ripe

2 packages instant vanilla pudding

1 can sweetened condensed milk

1 teaspoon vanilla extract

3 cups whole milk

1 12-oz. box Nilla Wafers

1 container Cool Whip

1 Add pudding, milk, and sweetened condensed milk to a bowl and whisk until thoroughly combined.

2 Add the vanilla extract and one cup of the Cool Whip to the bowl and whisk until combined.

3 Line the bottom of a bowl, or desired serving dish, with the Nilla Wafers. Slice bananas and place slices on top of Nilla Wafers. Cover banana slices and wafers with pudding. Repeat layering process until all the ingredients have been used.

4 Cover with leftover Cool Whip and sprinkle Nilla Wafer crumbs on top.

5 Place in refrigerator and chill for a minimum of five hours. For best results, chill overnight.

Pudding Pie

Easy and delicious!

1 Pour cream into bowl and whisk until soft peaks form. Be careful not to beat the cream too much, which will leave you with butter.

2 Place half the pudding into the piecrust.

3 Add half of the whipped cream to the pudding not in the piecrust. Pour this mixture on top of first layer of pudding.

4 Top with remaining whipped cream and place in refrigerator. Chill for a minimum of 15 minutes.

INGREDIENTS

1 chocolate cookie piecrust

2 cups heavy whipping cream

3 cups chocolate pudding, homemade or store-bought

Orsini Dirt

This recipe might just be my absolute favorite in the entire book. I was introduced to it a few years ago, by my friend Liz. Her mom sent it to her and she so graciously shared it with us. But be careful—having this in your possession is a little bit dangerous ...

INGREDIENTS

8 oz. of cream cheese

12 oz. of Cool Whip

¼ cup margarine

2 packages of instant French vanilla pudding

1 large package of Oreo cookies

1 cup powdered sugar

3 ½ cups whole milk

1 Place Oreos in a blender or food processor and process until finely crushed. It is OK if a few large pieces remain.

2 Add cream cheese, margarine, and sugar to separate bowl and mix until ingredients are thoroughly combined and fluffy.

3 Combine milk and pudding in a separate bowl and stir. When these have been combined, stir in Cool Whip.

4 Add pudding mixture to bowl containing the cream cheese mixture. Stir until thoroughly combined.

5 In a serving bowl, alternate layers of pudding/cream cheese mixture and Oreo crumbs until all ingredients have been used.

6 Place bowl in refrigerator and chill for at least one hour before serving.

Truffles

These are not the truffles you dig up in the forest with the help of a pig. These are great little bites to put out at any holiday party!

1 Heat the cream, vanilla extract, salt, and espresso grounds in a small saucepan over medium heat until the mixture is hot, but not boiling. As cream is warming, pour chocolate into bowl. Remove cream and pour over chocolate. Let stand 1-2 minutes and then stir until smooth. Refrigerate mixture for 40-50 minutes.

2 Line baking sheet with parchment paper. Remove chocolate mixture from refrigerator and use a small ice cream scoop or two spoons to remove small mounds of chocolate from the bowl. Place mounds onto baking sheet. When all of the chocolate has been used, place baking sheet in refrigerator for approximately 45 minutes, until mounds are firm.

3 Remove the baking sheet and gently roll mounds in your hands until they are tiny spheres. Roll spheres in topping of choice. Powdered sugar, finely chopped peanuts, almonds or pistachios, cocoa powder, toasted coconut, and rainbow sprinkles all produce lovely results. Return truffles to refrigerator and chill until ready to serve.

INGREDIENTS

16 oz. semi-sweet or dark chocolate pieces

1 cup heavy whipping cream

1 teaspoon pure vanilla extract

½ teaspoon sea salt

¼ teaspoon instant espresso grounds

Tiramisu

MAKES 8-10 SERVINGS • ACTIVE TIME: 30 MINUTES
TOTAL TIME: 4 HOURS AND 30 MINUTES

Tiramisu is the perfect dessert, as it combines coffee, chocolate, and cookies.

INGREDIENTS

2 cups freshly brewed espresso

½ cup sugar (plus 1 tablespoon)

3 tablespoons coffee liqueur

4 large egg yolks

⅓ cup dry Marsala wine

16 oz. mascarpone cheese

1 cup heavy whipping cream

36 ladyfingers

1 tablespoon unsweetened cocoa powder

1 Combine espresso, 1 tablespoon of sugar, and coffee liqueur in a bowl.

2 Add ½ cup of sugar, egg yolks, and Marsala wine to a bowl set over one inch of simmering water. Continually whisk the mixture until it its pale yellow and has almost tripled in size. This should take approximately 10 minutes. Remove bowl from heat and whisk in mascarpone cheese.

3 Place heavy cream in bowl and whisk until soft peaks begin to form. Gently fold the whipped cream into the mascarpone cheese mixture.

4 Submerge the ladyfingers in the espresso mixture and then cover the bottom of a nine-by-thirteen-inch baking dish with ladyfingers. You will use approximately half of the ladyfingers.

5 Spread half of the mascarpone mixture on top of the ladyfingers. Repeat Steps 4 and 5.

6 Cover with plastic and refrigerate for a minimum of three hours. Top with a sprinkle of unsweetened cocoa powder and whipped cream when ready to serve.

Crepes

MAKES 8-10 SERVINGS • ACTIVE TIME: 10 MINUTES
TOTAL TIME: 40-45 MINUTES

Crepes are a classic French food that you can find anywhere over there! These lovely pancakes can be either sweet or savory. Wrap some ham and cheese in one or cover one with chocolate hazelnut spread—either way is delicious! My preferred way to enjoy them is with a squeeze of lime juice and a generous sprinkle of sugar. It's simple and amazing!

1 Place all ingredients in a food processor and process until smooth.

2 Let batter stand at least 20 minutes. This ensures that all the ingredients are dissolved and that the batter will be completely smooth. The batter can also be refrigerated overnight.

3 Before using, whisk batter.

4 Lightly grease a small or medium frying pan with butter and place over medium heat.

5 Once the pan is heated, place about $1/3$ cup of batter into the center of the pan. While pouring, rock the pan in a circular motion so that the batter covers the bottom of the entire pan. You want the batter to lie as evenly as possible.

6 Let crepe cook for 2-3 minutes, until it is light brown. Use a spatula to loosen the crepe's edges and then flip it over. Cook until golden brown, approximately one more minute. Remove from pan.

Tip: Your first crepe might be a mess. Don't let this discourage you. This first crepe "seasoned the pan," so the rest will look great and taste even better!

INGREDIENTS

1 cup all-purpose flour

1½ cups whole milk

3 tablespoons melted butter

4 large eggs

1 tablespoons sugar

1 teaspoon honey

½ teaspoon sea salt

⅛ teaspoon freshly ground nutmeg

Oat Clusters

Bring these loaded clusters to your next tailgate. Simple to make and easy to transport.

1 Combine sugar, honey, salt, milk, butter, and cocoa powder in a saucepan and cook over medium heat. Once everything is dissolved and combined, cook for an additional 1-2 minutes.

2 Remove saucepan from heat and stir in the oats, peanut butter, and vanilla extract. Let cool for two minutes.

3 Line a baking sheet with parchment paper. Use tablespoon to scoop oat clusters onto baking sheet. Place in refrigerator and chill for one hour before serving.

INGREDIENTS

3 cups old-fashioned rolled oats

1 ½ cup sugar

¼ cup honey

1 cup creamy peanut butter

½ teaspoon sea salt

1 tablespoon pure vanilla extract

½ cup whole milk

1 stick butter

¼ cup unsweetened cocoa powder

Salted Caramels

**MAKES 30-40 CARAMELS • ACTIVE TIME: 45-50 MINUTES
TOTAL TIME: 3-4 HOURS**

Salted caramels are perfect for holiday gifts or parties. They are impressive, easy to eat—and better than any store-bought caramel out there.

INGREDIENTS

1 cup heavy whipping cream

2 teaspoons sea salt

5 tablespoons butter, softened

1 tablespoon bourbon

½ teaspoon pure vanilla extract

1 ½ cups sugar

¼ cup light corn syrup

¼ cup water

1 Place cream, salt, butter, bourbon, and vanilla in a small saucepan. Set aside.

2 Place sugar, corn syrup, and water into another saucepan. Cook over medium heat and do not stir. Instead, swirl the pan a few times and cook until mixture turns a light, golden brown.

3 Slowly pour the cream mixture into the pan containing the sugar. It will bubble furiously, but don't be afraid!

4 Insert candy thermometer in saucepan. Stir often and cook until thermometer reads between 245-250° F.

5 Remove saucepan from heat and pour contents into prepared baking dish. Sprinkle with sea salt. Allow to cool for a minimum of 2-3 hours before cutting and wrapping in parchment paper.

S'mores Muddy Buddies

MAKES 8-10 SERVINGS • ACTIVE TIME: 5 MINUTES
TOTAL TIME: 50 MINUTES

Save some for yourself, because they will be devoured in seconds when left unattended.

INGREDIENTS

9 cups Rice Chex

3 cups Golden Grahams cereal

1 cup mini-marshmallows

1 cup semi-sweet chocolate chips

¾ cup creamy peanut butter

1 teaspoon pure vanilla extract

1 ½ cups powdered sugar

1 Place chocolate chips and peanut butter in a microwave-safe bowl and microwave for 30 seconds. Remove from microwave, add vanilla and stir until mixture is smooth.

2 Place Chex in large bowl and pour chocolate-peanut butter mixture over the cereal. Carefully mix until the Chex are coated.

3 Place the Chex into a large plastic bag and add powdered sugar. Seal bag and shake until each piece is coated with sugar. Open the bag and add the Golden Grahams and marshmallows. Shake until everything is evenly distributed.

4 Line baking sheet with parchment paper and pour contents of bag onto baking sheet. Place sheet in refrigerator and chill for 30-45 minutes.

Muddy Buddies

**MAKES 8-10 SERVINGS • ACTIVE TIME: 5 MINUTES
TOTAL TIME: 50 MINUTES**

So easy to prepare, almost too easy to eat.

1 Place chocolate chips and peanut butter in a microwave-safe bowl and microwave for 30 seconds. Remove from microwave, add vanilla and stir until mixture is smooth.

2 Place Chex in large bowl and pour chocolate-peanut butter mixture over the cereal. Carefully mix until the Chex are coated.

3 Place the Chex into a large plastic bag and add powdered sugar. Seal bag and shake until each piece is coated with sugar.

4 Line baking sheet with parchment paper and pour Chex onto baking sheet. Place sheet in refrigerator and chill for 30-45 minutes.

INGREDIENTS

9 cups
Rice Chex

1 cup semi-sweet
chocolate chips

¾ cup creamy
peanut butter

1 teaspoon pure
vanilla extract

1 ½ cups
powdered sugar

Chocolate-Covered Popcorn

MAKES 10-12 SERVINGS • ACTIVE TIME: 10 MINUTES
TOTAL TIME: 40-45 MINUTES

A great sweet and savory treat for your next movie night.

INGREDIENTS

2 bags microwave popcorn, freshly popped

1 bag of white chocolate chips

1 bag of semi-sweet chocolate chips

½ teaspoon sea salt

¼ teaspoon freshly grated nutmeg

1 Place white chocolate chips in a microwave-safe bowl and microwave for 30 seconds. Remove and stir until smooth. Repeat for semi-sweet chocolate chips. If struggling to get chocolate smooth, return to microwave in 15-second intervals.

2 Open bags of popcorn and place each one in its own bowl. Add half of the salt and nutmeg to each and toss.

3 Drizzle the melted white chocolate over one bowl of popcorn. Drizzle the semi-sweet chocolate over the other.

4 Line baking sheet with parchment paper and pour popcorn onto baking sheet. Place sheet in refrigerator and chill for 30 minutes.

5 Once the chocolate has hardened, place all the popcorn in one large bowl and mix until evenly distributed. Then, enjoy!

Caramel Popcorn

MAKES 4-6 SERVINGS • ACTIVE TIME: 10 MINUTES
TOTAL TIME: 40-45 MINUTES

You definitely do not need to be on the boardwalk to enjoy this classic popcorn.

INGREDIENTS

1 bag of microwave popcorn, freshly popped

1 cup sugar

¼ cup water

3 tablespoons butter

½ teaspoon sea salt

1 Add the sugar, water, butter, and salt to a small saucepan and cook over medium-high heat until it is light brown. Be sure not to stir the mixture; instead, swirl the pan a few times as it cooks.

2 Reduce heat to medium and cook until mixture caramelizes, stirring once or twice. The mixture should take 3-5 minutes to caramelize.

3 Remove pan from heat and let cool for 30 seconds. Place popcorn in bowl and pour caramel over popcorn. Toss until popcorn is coated.

4 Line baking sheet with parchment paper and pour popcorn onto baking sheet. Let stand for 30 minutes before serving.

Affogato

Combine your coffee and dessert with this Italian classic!

1 Scoop ice cream into five small glasses. Pour one tablespoon of desired liqueur over each scoop. Grate nutmeg over each scoop. One or two passes over the grater for each is plenty.

2 Pour coffee or espresso over ice cream. Top with chocolate-covered espresso beans and whipped cream, if desired.

INGREDIENTS

1 pint vanilla ice cream

1½ cups brewed espresso or very strong coffee

5 tablespoons hazelnut liqueur, Kahlua, or Sambuca (anise liqueur)

Freshly grated nutmeg

Chocolate-covered espresso beans, crushed

Honeyed Walnuts
and Whipped Blue Cheese

**MAKES 4-6 SERVINGS • ACTIVE TIME: 10 MINUTES
TOTAL TIME: 10 MINUTES**

If classic sweets are not your thing, try this delectable blue cheese and walnut paring. The combination of sweet and savory is absolutely incredible.

INGREDIENTS

8 oz. blue cheese (Stilton or Point Reyes Original Blue)

¼ cup whole milk

¼ cup honey

1 cup walnuts

2 tablespoons butter

1 Place blue cheese and milk in a bowl and whisk until fluffy. Set bowl aside.

2 Place butter in a frying pan and cook over medium heat until melted. Add walnuts and cook until they are a light golden brown. Add the honey and cook for another two minutes.

3. Remove pan from heat and transfer contents to a bowl. Let walnuts cool. When ready to serve, spread blue cheese over crostini and top with warm walnuts.

Cinnamon Tortillas

MAKES 6-8 SERVINGS • ACTIVE TIME: 30 MINUTES
TOTAL TIME: 45 MINUTES

You likely have all of these ingredients in the house already. Fantastic little bites to satisfy any sweet tooth.

INGREDIENTS

10 small flour tortillas

1 cup sugar

¼ cup cinnamon

½ teaspoon freshly grated nutmeg

½ teaspoon sea salt

Vegetable oil

1 Cut the tortillas into strips, then cut the strips in half.

2 Heat 4-5 inches of vegetable oil in a large saucepan over medium-high heat. When it's hot, drop a handful of the tortilla strips in and fry for 2-3 minutes or until they turn a light golden brown. Remove from oil and dry on a paper towel-lined cooling rack.

3 While tortillas are cooling, mix sugar, cinnamon, nutmeg, and salt in a bowl. Place still warm tortillas in the bowl, toss until coated evenly, and serve!

Filo-Wrapped Mozzarella
with Honey Glaze

MAKES 8 SERVINGS • ACTIVE TIME: 10-15 MINUTES
TOTAL TIME: 15-20 MINUTES

This dessert is perfect for those who don't have the biggest sweet tooth. The honey adds just a touch of sweetness—the perfect compliment to the salty cheese!

INGREDIENTS

8 sheets of filo dough

8 oz. mozzarella cheese

1 cup honey

1 tablespoon black sesame seeds, toasted

Vegetable oil

1 In a large saucepan, heat six inches of vegetable oil over medium high-heat until it reaches approximately 350° F.

2 Cut the mozzarella into eight one-ounce slices. Wrap each slice of cheese in one sheet of filo dough. You want to wrap the cheese like a burrito, tucking in the sides to make sure the cheese does not escape once it is melted.

3 Place two or three of the mozzarella wraps into the oil and fry for 2-3 minutes, or until the dough is a light golden brown and crispy. Remove from oil and let stand on a paper towel-lined cooling rack. Repeat until all eight wraps have been fried.

4 Place the sesame seeds in a small saucepan and toast very lightly, 15-30 seconds over medium heat. Add the honey and warm until it begins to loosen. Place each mozzarella wrap onto a serving plate and drizzle honey-sesame seed mixture over the top. Then pour the remaining honey-sesame seed mixture into a bowl for dipping, and serve!

S'mores with Cheese

These cheesy s'mores will forever change your idea of the campfire classic!

INGREDIENTS

- 8 oz. sharp cheddar cheese
- 8 graham crackers
- 2 chocolate bars (semi-sweet or milk chocolate)

1 Break graham crackers in half, creating 16 pieces. Place on a baking sheet.

2 Cut cheese into eight 1-inch slices and break the chocolate into eight pieces.

3 Place the cheese on the cracker. Transfer the cracker and cheese onto a foil-lined grill over medium-high heat. Cover and let the cheese melt for 4-5 minutes. Once melted, remove cracker from grill, top with chocolate and top with another graham cracker.

Chocolate-Covered Pretzels

MAKES 4-6 SERVINGS • ACTIVE TIME: 10-15 MINUTES
TOTAL TIME: 1 HOUR AND 15 MINUTES

Whether you choose pretzel rods or twists, these little treats are perfect for any of the dessert dips.

INGREDIENTS

20 long pretzel sticks
or 50 classic pretzel twists

2 cups semi-sweet chocolate chips

1 tablespoon butter

1 Place chocolate in a microwave-safe bowl and microwave on high in 15-second intervals until chocolate is melted. Be sure to check bowl each time to ensure that the chocolate does not get overcooked. You want the melted chocolate to look glossy and smooth. Add the butter and stir until combined.

2 Dip half of the pretzel into the chocolate. Line a baking sheet with wax paper and place coated pretzels onto sheet. Once all pretzels have been used, place the baking sheet in the refrigerator for a minimum of one hour, or until the chocolate is set.

Panna Cotta

MAKES 8 SERVINGS • ACTIVE TIME: 20 MINUTES
TOTAL TIME: 2-3 HOURS

You may have seen panna cotta on the menu at all kinds of restaurants. Well, now you can easily whip it up at home!

INGREDIENTS

1 package unflavored gelatin

2 teaspoons cold water

2 cups heavy whipping cream

1 cup half-and-half

⅓ cup sugar

1 ½ teaspoons pure vanilla extract

½ teaspoon freshly grated nutmeg

¼ teaspoon ground cardamom

1 Combine water and gelatin in saucepan and let stand until gelatin dissolves.

2 In a separate saucepan, combine the cream, half-and-half, and sugar. Warm over medium heat until hot but not boiling. Once mixture is hot, add gelatin, vanilla, nutmeg, and cardamom.

3 Pour mixture into ramekins and place in refrigerator.

4 When ready to serve, dip each dish ¾ of the way into a bowl of hot water and run a paring knife around the edge of the ramekin for easy removal. Flip dish over and place onto plate. Top with berry compote or maple syrup, or serve plain.

Cheesecake

Top this tasty treat with fresh fruit, a berry compote, or whipped cream!

1 Place graham crackers in a food processor and process until finely ground. Add brown sugar and melted butter, and mix together until well combined. Press this mixture into the bottom of a springform pan, allowing it to go up an inch or two on the sides. Make sure to press in an even flat layer. Place pan in freezer.

2 Place the sweetened condensed milk, vanilla, nutmeg, and cream cheese in the bowl of an electric mixer and mix until smooth. Add the lemon juice and beat until thoroughly combined.

3 Pour cream cheese mixture into the springform pan and cover directly with plastic wrap.

4 Place in the refrigerator for a minimum of 3-4 hours before serving.

INGREDIENTS

20 graham crackers

2 tablespoons light brown sugar

1 can sweetened condensed milk

1 teaspoon pure vanilla extract

½ teaspoon freshly ground nutmeg

2 8-oz. packages of cream cheese

1½ sticks of butter, melted

¼ cup freshly squeezed lemon juice

Fresh fruit and powdered sugar, for garnish

Cheesecake Parfait

MAKES 8-10 SERVINGS • ACTIVE TIME: 30 MINUTES
TOTAL TIME: 1 HOUR

A parfait is an easy way to avoid the mess that slicing up a cake can produce. I like to add extra graham crackers to mine!

INGREDIENTS

20 graham crackers

Preferred fresh fruit

2 tablespoons light brown sugar

1 can sweetened condensed milk

1 teaspoon pure vanilla extract

½ teaspoon freshly ground nutmeg

2 8-oz. packages of cream cheese

1½ sticks butter

¼ cup freshly squeezed lemon juice

1 Place graham crackers in a food processor and process until finely ground. Add brown sugar and melted butter, and mix together until well combined.

2 Place the sweetened condensed milk, vanilla, nutmeg, and cream cheese in the bowl of an electric mixer and mix until smooth. Add the lemon juice and beat until thoroughly combined.

3 Layer the graham cracker crumbs, fresh fruit, and cheesecake mixture in tall glasses or mason jars. Fill containers to the top and cover directly with plastic wrap.

4 Place in the refrigerator and chill for at least 30 minutes, then serve!

French Silk Parfait

French silk pie is a classic. Save time by eliminating the crust!

1 Place the graham crackers and granulated sugar in food processor and process until both are finely ground.

2 Place the cream cheese, vanilla, and powdered sugar in a bowl and beat until combined. Chop up the chocolate and place in a microwave-safe bowl with butter. Microwave on high for 30 seconds and mix. If not smooth, return to microwave for another 15 seconds. Let cool for a few seconds and then add chocolate to cream cheese mixture. Beat until well combined and then gently fold in three cups of the whipped cream.

3 Layer the graham crackers, chocolate, and whipped cream in mason jars or tall glasses, making sure to end with a layer of whipped cream on top . Sprinkle chocolate shavings on top, place in the refrigerator for at least 30 minutes, and then serve.

INGREDIENTS

20 graham crackers

1 tablespoon sugar

8 oz. cream cheese

1 teaspoon pure vanilla extract

2 oz. German chocolate

2 oz. unsweetened Baker's chocolate

4 tablespoons butter

2 cups powdered sugar

5 cups whipped cream, divided: 3 for filling, 2 for layering (whipped cream recipe page 248)

Chocolate shavings

Honey Peanut Truffles

There is no better combo than peanut butter and honey. It's the perfect mix of sweet and salty.

INGREDIENTS

½ cup peanut butter

¼ cup honey

¼ teaspoon sea salt

1 cup rolled oats, finely ground

½ cup semi-sweet chocolate chips, melted

1 In a food processor, grind the oats until they are very fine. Add the peanut butter, honey, and salt, and blend until well combined. Line a baking sheet with parchment paper, scoop out teaspoon-sized balls of the peanut butter mixture and place on sheet. Place sheet into refrigerator for one hour.

2 Place chocolate chips in microwave-safe bowl and microwave for 15-20 seconds, or until chocolate is melted. Mix chocolate until smooth, and then remove the baking sheet from the refrigerator. Drizzle the chocolate over the truffles or dip the truffles halfway into the chocolate. Place truffles back into the refrigerator until chocolate is set.

Chocolate Mousse

**MAKES 5-6 SERVINGS • ACTIVE TIME: 15 MINUTES
TOTAL TIME: 1 HOUR AND 15 MINUTES**

Chocolate mousse is one of my favorite desserts of all-time. It's light and airy, but still packs tons of chocolate flavor!

1 Place the chocolate in a microwave-safe bowl and microwave on high for 25-35 seconds. Mix until smooth. If chocolate is not completely melted, return to microwave for a few more seconds, but be careful to not overcook.

2 Place the cream in a bowl and whip until soft peaks form. Place the sugar, egg whites, vanilla, and salt in a separate bowl and stir until peaks form.

3 Slowly add the chocolate to the egg white mixture and stir until almost completely combined. Gently fold in the whipped cream. Dollop mousse into serving dishes and refrigerate for at least one hour. Top with homemade whipped cream, mint, fresh fruit, or chocolate shavings when ready to serve.

INGREDIENTS

2 cups heavy whipping cream, cold

1 cup bittersweet chocolate

2 tablespoons sugar

3 egg whites

½ teaspoon pure vanilla extract

¼ teaspoon sea salt

Chewy Peanut Butter Oat Bars

MAKES 10-12 BARS • ACTIVE TIME: 15 MINUTES
TOTAL TIME: 45 MINUTES

These are great to bring to tailgates as they are simple and travel well. I absolutely love these little bars!

INGREDIENTS

¾ cup milk

1 cup sugar

¼ teaspoon sea salt

1 teaspoon pure vanilla extract

1 oz. dark chocolate, melted

½ cup creamy peanut butter

⅔ cup quick cooking oats

¼ cup old-fashioned rolled oats

1 Place the milk, sugar, and salt in a small saucepan and whisk them together. Cook over medium heat until mixture thickens and comes to a boil, approximately 10 minutes. Remove pan from heat.

2 Add vanilla, chocolate, and peanut butter to pan and mix until well combined. Fold in all of the oats and mix until they are completely coated.

3 Line an eight-by-eight-inch baking pan with parchment paper and pour contents of saucepan into it. Press into an even layer and let bars sit for 30 minutes. You want them to be firm and not break when picked up. Cut into little bars and serve immediately, or store in the refrigerator.

Tapioca Pudding

MAKES 6 SERVINGS • ACTIVE TIME: 25 MINUTES
TOTAL TIME: 30 MINUTES

Top tapioca pudding with fresh fruit and honey for added freshness!

INGREDIENTS

2 large eggs

1 cup sugar

½ cup quick cooking tapioca

1 vanilla bean, cut lengthwise

4 cups half-and-half

1 teaspoon pure vanilla extract

½ teaspoon sea salt

¼ teaspoon freshly ground nutmeg

1 Place the eggs, sugar, tapioca, and vanilla bean in a medium saucepan and whisk until the mixture is pale yellow and frothy.

2 Add the half-and-half and simmer over medium-high heat while stirring constantly. Cook for approximately 10 minutes or until mixture is very thick.

3 Remove the vanilla bean and mix in the vanilla extract.

4 Remove from heat and transfer to a bowl. Let cool for at least four hours before serving.

Chocolate-Coffee Truffles

MAKES 30-40 TRUFFLES • ACTIVE TIME: 15 MINUTES
TOTAL TIME: 4 HOURS AND 15 MINUTES

Coffee brings out the rich flavor of chocolate. Sounds a bit odd, but you will see what I mean. They are super chocolaty!

1 Place coffee beans in a food processor and process until finely ground.

2 Place cream, amaretto, and salt in a small saucepan and cook over medium heat until hot, but not boiling. Once hot, remove from heat and pour over the chocolate. Let stand for 2-3 minutes and then stir until smooth. Let chocolate chill in refrigerator for at least three hours.

3 Line a baking sheet with parchment paper. Remove chocolate from refrigerator, remove in teaspoon-sized scoops and roll these into spheres. Roll chocolate in ground coffee beans and then place onto the baking sheet. Place in the refrigerator for at least one hour before serving.

INGREDIENTS

9 oz. bittersweet chocolate, chopped

1 cup heavy whipping cream

4 tablespoons amaretto liqueur

¼ teaspoon sea salt

¾ cup chocolate-covered coffee beans

Rice Pudding

**MAKES 6-8 SERVINGS • ACTIVE TIME: 30 MINUTES
TOTAL TIME: 30-35 MINUTES**

There is truly nothing better than rice pudding during the holidays. Whether you serve it warm or chilled, it is the perfect post-dinner treat.

INGREDIENTS

4 ½ cups whole milk

½ cup heavy cream

1 cup arborio rice

½ cup sugar

1 teaspoon ground cinnamon

½ teaspoon freshly grated nutmeg

3 strips of orange zest (use vegetable peeler)

1 vanilla bean, halved lengthwise or 1 teaspoon pure vanilla extract

½ teaspoon sea salt

1 egg yolk

1 Combine milk, cream, rice, sugar, orange zest, cinnamon, nutmeg, vanilla, and salt in a medium saucepan and bring to a light boil. Reduce heat to low and cook for approximately 25 minutes, until rice is tender and mixture is thick. Stir while cooking to make sure rice doesn't stick to the bottom of the pan.

2 Remove from heat and remove the orange zest and vanilla bean, if used. Let stand for 3-5 minutes. Whisk in the egg yolk quickly until very well combined. Serve warm or place in refrigerator. When ready to serve, a bit of nutmeg, cinnamon, or slivered almonds make nice toppings.

Fruit

These days, you can get fruit in every season. But when you're deciding on what to make for dessert, consider what is fresh, in-season, and readily available at your local farmers' market. Something as simple as a fruit salad is perfect year-round, because you can easily adjust the ingredients to fit what is available. For instance, in the fall you can use ripe apples, pears, grapes, and pomegranate seeds to match the colors of the foliage. In the weeks before the 4th of July, collect as many berries as you can and toss them into everything. And don't worry about going overboard—you can always freeze berries for those cold winter months when you need to be reminded of the summer. Fruit makes dessert a cinch, so long as you remember this: The fresher the fruit, the better the dessert!

Classic Summer Fruit Salad

Yep, here it is! A refreshing conclusion to the hamburgers, hot dogs, and potato salad.

INGREDIENTS

1 pint strawberries, halved

1 pint blueberries

1 pint raspberries

2 cups seedless grapes (red or green), halved

5 fresh mint leaves, finely chopped

¼ cup freshly squeezed orange juice

1 teaspoon honey

1 Add mint, orange juice, and honey to a bowl and stir together. Set bowl aside.

2 In a separate bowl, mix strawberries, blueberries, blackberries, raspberries, and grapes together. Add dressing and toss.

3 Place in refrigerator and chill for 20 minutes before serving.

Tropical Fruit Salad

MAKES 10-12 SERVINGS • ACTIVE TIME: 10 MINUTES
TOTAL TIME: 10 MINUTES

Want to get away? A salad with ripe tropical fruit will instantly transport you to a warm, breezy island.

1 Combine lime zest, lime juice, mint, and honey in a small bowl. Set aside.

2 Combine fruit in large bowl. Add dressing and toss. Serve immediately.

INGREDIENTS

4 kiwis, peeled and sliced

1 pineapple, cubed

1 mango, cubed

1 cup strawberries, sliced

2 cups seedless grapes (red or green), halved

1 cup blueberries

Zest of 1 lime

Juice of 1 lime

¼ cup fresh mint, chopped

1 tablespoon honey

Melon Fruit Salad

I always have so much fun using a melon baller. The little spheres make for a cute and creative salad.

INGREDIENTS

1 cantaloupe

1 honeydew melon

½ watermelon

¼ cup lime juice

2 tablespoons honey

¼ cup fresh mint, chopped

1 Use a melon baller and scoop out the insides of the cantaloupe, the honeydew melon, and the watermelon. Place melon balls in a large bowl.

2 Combine lime juice, honey, and mint in a separate bowl.

3 Add dressing to bowl containing melon balls. Toss and serve immediately.

Citrus Fruit Salad

MAKES 6-8 SERVINGS • **ACTIVE TIME: 10 MINUTES**
TOTAL TIME: 10 MINUTES

Tart, sweet, and zesty!

1 To segment the citrus fruits, use a paring knife to remove the peel and the pith. Cut out the natural segments and place in a large bowl. When fruit has been removed, squeeze the juice remaining in the citrus membranes into a separate bowl.

2 Add the lime zest, lime juice, mint, and sugar to the bowl containing the citrus juices. Stir to combine.

3 Add dressing to bowl containing citrus pieces. Toss and serve immediately.

INGREDIENTS

4 oranges, segmented

2 grapefruits, segmented

6 clementines, segmented

2 blood oranges, segmented

¼ cup fresh mint, chopped

Zest of 1 lime

Juice of 1 lime

1 teaspoon sugar

Pomegranate seeds, for garnish

Watermelon & Mozzarella Fruit Salad

MAKES 6-8 SERVINGS • ACTIVE TIME: 10 MINUTES
TOTAL TIME: 10 MINUTES

Reminiscent of a caprese salad, but the watermelon is a bit more subtle than the tomato. Yum!

INGREDIENTS

8 oz. fresh mozzarella cheese

½ fresh watermelon

3 tablespoons extra virgin olive oil

3 tablespoons balsamic glaze

1 teaspoon sea salt

1 teaspoon freshly ground black pepper

10 leaves fresh baby basil, chopped

1 Cut mozzarella into eight thin slices.

2 Cut watermelon into slices that are approximately ¹/₂-inch thick.

3 Overlap alternating slices of mozzarella and watermelon on a platter.

4 Drizzle with extra virgin olive oil and balsamic glaze.

5 Sprinkle with salt, pepper, and basil. Serve immediately.

Strawberries and Cream Trifle

MAKES 4-6 SERVINGS • ACTIVE TIME: 45 MINUTES
TOTAL TIME: 45 MINUTES

I like to serve a trifle like this when I need something beautiful that is both easy to prepare and delicious.

1 Place strawberries, lemon juice, sugar, and cornstarch in a medium saucepan and cook over medium heat until strawberries soften and begin to give up their juice, approximately five minutes. Remove from heat and let cool.

2 Add whipped cream, powdered sugar, and vanilla extract to bowl. Whisk until soft peaks form. Very gently fold the lemon curd into the whipped cream.

3 Cut the pound cake into slices that are approximately $1/2$-inch thick.

4 Cover bottom of trifle dish with lemon whipped cream. Place layer of pound cake slices on top and then scoop berry mixture on top of pound cake. Repeat until all the strawberries and pound cake have been used, giving you three or four layers. Top with remaining lemon whipped cream.

5 Place in refrigerator until ready to serve!

Variation: Feel free to add in any of your favorite berries, such as blueberries, raspberries, or blackberries!

INGREDIENTS

4 pints strawberries

Juice of 1 lemon

3 tablespoons sugar

1 teaspoon cornstarch

1 quart heavy whipping cream

1 tablespoon powdered sugar

1 teaspoon pure vanilla extract

12 oz. lemon curd (homemade or store-bought)

1 pound cake (homemade or store-bought)

Bananas Foster

MAKES 2 SERVINGS • ACTIVE TIME: 10 MINUTES
TOTAL TIME: 10 MINUTES

Once you've tried making this once or twice, you'll realize how easy it is. This is a great recipe to prepare with some friends in the kitchen—you'll look like a pro!

INGREDIENTS

1 tablespoon butter

1 tablespoon dark brown sugar

1 banana, peeled and halved lengthwise

1 teaspoon cinnamon

½ teaspoon freshly ground nutmeg

¼ cup light rum

1 Place butter and sugar in a medium frying pan and heat until melted. Add the bananas and cook until they are a light golden brown all over. You will have to flip the bananas once or twice. Add the spices and cook for 1-2 more minutes. Turn off the burner.

2 Add the rum and light the sauce on fire with a match. Be very careful here and stand back, as the flame can be quite large. As the flame is burning, spoon the sauce over the bananas. Do this until the flame dissipates completely. Transfer to serving dishes and enjoy with ice cream or as is!

Jello

Jello is wiggly and whimsical! Using fresh fruit juice to customize the flavor makes all the difference. Try pomegranate juice or coconut water for creative new flavor choices.

INGREDIENTS

2 cups fruit juice (i.e. cranberry, apple, etc.)

2 tablespoons of unflavored gelatin

1 tablespoon honey

1 Combine all ingredients in a saucepan and simmer for approximately 10 minutes.

2 Remove from heat and cool for no more than 1 ¹/₂ minutes.

3 Pour into serving dishes, a bowl, or ice cube trays and let chill for a minimum of five hours or overnight.

Lemon Curd

Serve this tart and whimsical curd with scones and small cakes during afternoon tea! This curd can also be topped with meringue and put under a broiler to make lemon meringue pie.

INGREDIENTS

½ cup freshly squeezed lemon juice

2 teaspoons lemon zest

3 large eggs

⅔ cup sugar

1 stick butter

1 Combine ingredients in a standing mixer and mix until well combined. Pour mixture into saucepan and cook over low heat until it has thickened, approximately 10 minutes.

2 Pour into serving dish and place in refrigerator. Chill until it thickens further. Curd can be served with fruit, gingersnaps, or graham crackers.

Key Lime Pie Curd

MAKES 4-5 SERVINGS • ACTIVE TIME: 15 MINUTES
TOTAL TIME: 1 HOUR AND 15 MINUTES

Key limes are different from regular limes, in that they are a bit more tart and floral. This curd is amazing with some fresh fruit, and compliments just about anything.

INGREDIENTS

2 tablespoons key lime zest

1 cup key lime juice

1 cup sugar

½ teaspoon sea salt

3 tablespoons cornstarch

1 stick butter, softened

5 large egg yolks

1 In a medium saucepan, combine lime zest, lime juice, sugar, salt, and cornstarch and cook over medium-high heat, whisking constantly, until the sugar is dissolved and ingredients are combined.

2 Place egg yolks in a bowl and beat. Add a small amount of the lime mixture and whisk until yolks are tempered. This prevents the eggs from becoming scrambled when added to the curd.

3 Add the yolks to the saucepan, stirring constantly while pouring. Reduce heat to low and cook until the curd is thick and smooth.

4 Remove from heat and allow to cool. Place plastic directly on curd's surface and refrigerate. Serve with fresh fruit, shortbread cookies, or even scones!

Berry Compote

Berry compotes are perfect over vanilla ice cream, spread on top of challah bread, or French toast. And if you're really adventurous, try making a PB&J with this stuff!

INGREDIENTS

1 cup blueberries

1 cup blackberries

1 cup raspberries

½ cup strawberries

⅓ cup light brown sugar

4 tablespoons butter

1 tablespoon honey

½ teaspoon sea salt

3 tablespoons freshly squeezed lemon juice

1 teaspoon lemon zest

1 Place butter in a medium saucepan and cook over medium heat until melted. Add berries, brown sugar, honey, and salt and stir. Cook for 5-6 minutes while mashing the berries to help the juices release.

2 Add lemon juice and lemon zest and cook for another two minutes. Remove from heat and let stand for 3-4 minutes. Compote can be served warm or placed in refrigerator until ready to serve.

Ambrosia

MAKES 6-8 SERVINGS • ACTIVE TIME: 20 MINUTES
TOTAL TIME: 3 HOURS AND 20 MINUTES

This recipe is definitely something your grandparents were making for parties. But even though it's old school, the deliciousness stands the test of time!

1 Place whipping cream and sugar in a bowl and whisk until stiff peaks begin to form. Whisk in the sour cream and nutmeg.

2 Add the mini-marshmallows, fruit, coconut, nuts, and cherries to the bowl. Cover and let chill for a minimum of three hours before serving.

INGREDIENTS

½ cup heavy whipping cream

1 tablespoon sugar

½ cup sour cream

¼ teaspoon freshly grated nutmeg

3 cups mini-marshmallows

6 clementines, segmented

1 cup pineapple, cubed

1 cup coconut, grated

1 cup toasted pecans, chopped

¾ cup maraschino cherries

Nutella Dumplings with Strawberries

MAKES 30 DUMPLINGS • ACTIVE TIME: 45 MINUTES
TOTAL TIME: 45 MINUTES

Dumplings are not commonly on dessert lists, but these little treats are the perfect finger food if you're doing tapas-style desserts.

INGREDIENTS

30 wonton wrappers

30 teaspoons nutella (homemade or store-bought)

1 pint fresh strawberries

Vegetable oil

Powdered sugar

1 Heat 4-5 inches of vegetable oil in a large frying pan over medium-high heat.

2 Lay out the wonton wrappers and place one teaspoon of Nutella and a few pieces of strawberry in the wonton's center.

3 To seal the wonton, dip your finger in water and run the water along the wonton's outer edge. Pull one side over the other to form a triangle and seal the wonton. Try to keep out as much air as possible, but don't let any filling escape. Wrap the wonton's edges over one another to seal more securely.

4 Once the oil is heated, place 3-4 wontons into the pan and fry for 2-3 minutes. Flip them over in order to ensure that they are being cooked evenly.

5 Remove wontons from oil and drain on a paper towel-lined cooling rack. When dry but still warm, sprinkle with a little powdered sugar and serve!

Blueberry Mascarpone Dumplings

MAKES 30 DUMPLINGS • ACTIVE TIME: 45 MINUTES
TOTAL TIME: 45 MINUTES

Little bundles of joy!

1 Heat 4-5 inches of vegetable oil in a large frying pan over medium-high heat.

2 Lay out the wonton wrappers and place one teaspoon of mascarpone and a few blueberries in the wonton's center.

3 To seal the wonton, dip your finger in water and run the water along the wonton's outer edge. Pull one side over the other to form a triangle and seal the wonton. Try to keep out as much air as possible, but don't let any filling escape. Wrap the wonton's edges over one another to seal more securely.

4 Once the oil is heated, place 3-4 wontons into the pan and fry for 2-3 minutes. Flip them in order to ensure that they are being cooked evenly.

5 Remove wontons from oil and drain on a paper towel-lined cooling rack. When dry but still warm, sprinkle with a little powdered sugar and serve!

INGREDIENTS

30 wonton wrappers

30 teaspoons mascarpone cheese

1 pint fresh blueberries

Vegetable oil

Powdered sugar

Macerated Strawberries

MAKES 4 SERVINGS • ACTIVE TIME: 5 MINUTES
TOTAL TIME: 2 HOURS AND 5 MINUTES

Serve these with a big bowl of whipped cream or scooped over fresh pound cake.

INGREDIENTS

1 pint fresh strawberries, quartered

1 tablespoon freshly squeezed lemon juice

3 tablespoons sugar

1 Combine all ingredients in a bowl. Toss a few times until strawberries are evenly coated.

2 Place bowl in the refrigerator and chill for 1-2 hours. The strawberries are ready to serve when their juices start to release, creating a little strawberry sauce.

Apricots with Moscato Reduction

MAKES 6-8 SERVINGS • ACTIVE TIME: 15 MINUTES
TOTAL TIME: 10-12 HOURS

Thyme complements the fresh flavors of the apricots in this recipe—and the Moscato D'Asti adds a sweetness that you can't get from sugar!

1 Bring the Moscato to boil in a small saucepan. Remove pan from heat and add the dried apricots. Cover pan and let stand for at least 10 hours. Strain wine into a bowl and reserve one cup of the liquid. Reserve the dried apricots as well.

2 Bring the reserved cup of Moscato and the sugar to a boil in a small saucepan. Once the sugar has dissolved, add the thyme and simmer for 10 minutes. Remove pan from heat and remove the thyme. Let cool in the refrigerator.

3 Slice the rehydrated apricots into pieces and cut up the fresh apricots. Place apricot pieces into a bowl and pour syrup over the top. Toss to coat. Serve plain, or with vanilla ice cream.

INGREDIENTS

3 cups Moscato D'Asti (use one you would drink)

20 dried apricots

⅓ cup sugar

½ teaspoon freshly grated nutmeg

2 sprigs fresh thyme

16 fresh apricots

Chai-Poached Pears

MAKES 4 SERVINGS • ACTIVE TIME: 50 MINUTES
TOTAL TIME: 1 HOUR AND 20 MINUTES

Chai can act as a flavorful poaching liquid that pairs beautifully with sweet pears. Serve with a little cinnamon whipped cream on top if you have time!

INGREDIENTS

2 cups water

2 bags of chai tea

1 cinnamon stick

3 whole cloves

1 teaspoon freshly grated nutmeg

2 ripe pears, peeled and cored

1 In a small saucepan, bring the water to a boil. Add the tea bags and spices and reduce the heat so that the water is simmering. Simmer for 10 minutes, turn off heat and let everything steep for 30 minutes.

2 Remove spices and tea bags from the water. Add sugar and stir over low heat until the sugar is dissolved. Place the pears into the simmering tea and cook until pears are tender, approximately 40 minutes. Make sure to turn the pears over a few times to ensure that they are cooked. To test doneness, poke the thickest part of the pear. The pear should slip right off the knife when it is ready. Remove pears from liquid and serve with cinnamon whipped cream.

Chocolate-Covered Strawberries

This classic is decadent and tasty. Serve at a dinner party or keep them all for yourself!

1 Wash the strawberries and pat them dry.

2 Place chocolate chips in a microwave-safe bowl and microwave on high for 25-35 seconds. Remove from microwave and mix until smooth. Dip each strawberry into the chocolate halfway, or completely, whichever you prefer. If desired, roll chocolate-covered strawberries in graham cracker crumbs or the ground almonds.

3 Line a baking sheet with parchment paper and place strawberries on sheet. Place strawberries in the refrigerator for at least two hours before serving.

INGREDIENTS

1 pint fresh strawberries

1 cup semi-sweet chocolate chips

3 graham crackers, crushed

½ cup blanched almonds, finely ground

Cheesecake-Filled Strawberries

MAKES 20-25 STRAWBERRIES • ACTIVE TIME: 25 MINUTES
TOTAL TIME: 1 HOUR AND 25 MINUTES

These bite-sized cheesecakes are perfect for a Spanish-tapas style dessert! They're delicious, easy to eat, and, best of all, there's no dishes to wash after.

INGREDIENTS

1-2 pints fresh strawberries

8 oz. cream cheese

½ cup powdered sugar

1 teaspoon pure vanilla extract

¼ teaspoon salt

⅓ cup heavy whipping cream

4 graham crackers, ground

1 Wash the strawberries and dry completely. Remove the stems and scoop out the core with a spoon. Make sure there is enough room for a little bit of filling in each strawberry.

2 In the bowl of an electric mixer, beat the heavy cream until soft peaks form.

3 Add the cream cheese, sugar, vanilla, and salt, and mix until light and fluffy. Place mixture into a plastic bag or a piping bag. If using a plastic bag, cut a small opening in one of the bottom corners and squeeze the mixture into the cavity you made in the strawberries. You want the filling to form a mound on top of the strawberries without overflowing. Sprinkle graham crackers crumbs on top and then place in the refrigerator for one hour before serving.

Limoncello Fruit Salad

Limoncello adds another level to the lemon flavor in this fruit salad. The three lemon aspects brighten the summer fruit and enhance their fresh flavors, making this fruit salad the perfect end to any meal.

INGREDIENTS

1 pint strawberries, quartered

1 pint blueberries

1 pint blackberries

1 teaspoon lemon zest

1 tablespoon freshly squeezed lemon juice

¼ cup limoncello

2 tablespoons sugar

¼ cup mint, chopped

Toss all ingredients in a bowl and let stand for 5 minutes before serving!

Cherry Compote

MAKES 1 ½ CUPS • ACTIVE TIME: 15 MINUTES
TOTAL TIME: 20 MINUTES

Cherry compote is a perfect topping for Greek yogurt, pound cake, or vanilla ice cream. This recipe is great for when you have extra cherries that need to be used up!

INGREDIENTS

1 lb. fresh cherries, pits removed

1 tablespoon lemon zest

3 tablespoons sugar

¼ teaspoon sea salt

1 Place the cherries, sugar, and salt in a medium saucepan and cook over low heat until the juices have released and thickened, and the fruit is tender. You want the juice to coat the back of a spoon. This should take approximately 10 minutes.

2 During the final two minutes, add the lemon zest. Remove saucepan from heat and serve warm, or place in the refrigerator.

Fig-and-Port Reduction

MAKES 4-6 SERVINGS • ACTIVE TIME: 25 MINUTES

Port isn't just for drinking alongside your dessert. Reducing it with fresh figs helps concentrate all of the complex flavors in the wine.

1 Place the port and sugar in a medium saucepan and cook over medium-low heat until sugar is dissolved. Add the cloves, nutmeg and figs to the pan. Cook until the port has been reduced by half. This should take anywhere from 10-20 minutes.

2 Place the water and cornstarch in a small bowl and mix until well combined.

3 Slowly pour the cornstarch mixture into the port while whisking constantly. Cook this mixture for five minutes, or until slightly thickened.

4 Remove pan from heat and let stand for five minutes. Serve over ice cream, yogurt, pound cake, cheesecake, etc.

INGREDIENTS

1 cup ripe figs, halved

2 cups tawny port

½ cup sugar

½ teaspoon freshly ground nutmeg

3 whole cloves

1 tablespoon water

2 teaspoons cornstarch

Strawberry-Rhubarb Compote

MAKES 3 CUPS • ACTIVE TIME: 20 MINUTES
TOTAL TIME: 2 HOURS AND 20 MINUTES

Serve this sweet-and-tart compote with angel food cake or cheesecake!

INGREDIENTS

4 cups rhubarb, sliced

4 cups fresh strawberries, sliced

½ cup sugar

2 tablespoons water

½ teaspoon pure vanilla extract

½ teaspoon sea salt

½ teaspoon freshly grated nutmeg

1 Combine the rhubarb, strawberries, sugar, water, and salt in a medium saucepan and bring to a boil.

2 Reduce heat to low and cook until rhubarb and berries are tender. This should take approximately 5-10 minutes.

3 Once tender, remove from heat and stir the vanilla and nutmeg into the pan.

4 Place in the refrigerator for a minimum of two hours before serving.

Pineapple-Coconut Cream

MAKES 4-6 SERVINGS • ACTIVE TIME: 10 MINUTES
TOTAL TIME: 10 MINUTES

This whimsical recipe is like eating a pineapple-coconut cloud!

1 Place the cream cheese and Cool Whip in a bowl and beat until light and fluffy. Mix in the vanilla.

2 Drain the pineapple, making sure to squeeze out as much liquid as possible.

3 Fold the pineapple and coconut into the cream cheese-Cool Whip mixture. Scoop into serving dishes and top with macadamia nuts.

INGREDIENTS

8 oz. cream cheese

2 cups Cool Whip

1 can crushed pineapple, drained

½ teaspoon pure vanilla extract

½ cup shredded coconut, sweetened

½ cup macadamia nuts, chopped

Strawberry Daiquiri

This drink is fun and refreshing. In other words, it's perfect for summer!

INGREDIENTS

1 bag frozen strawberries

½ cup freshly squeezed lime juice

¼ cup sugar

1 tablespoon honey

⅓ cup light rum, optional

1 Place all ingredients in a blender and blend until smooth.

2 Pour into tall glasses and top with a fresh strawberry and a sprig of fresh mint.

Piña Colada

This piña colada will transport you right to the tropics!

1 Place all ingredients in a blender and blend until smooth.

2 Pour into tall glasses and serve with a straw.

INGREDIENTS

½ fresh pineapple, cubed and frozen

1 cup ice

¼ cup pineapple juice

¼ cup coconut cream

2 tablespoons white rum

1 tablespoon dark rum

½ teaspoon freshly grated nutmeg

Candied Plantains

MAKES 4 SERVINGS • ACTIVE TIME: 5 MINUTES
TOTAL TIME: 8-10 MINUTES

Reminiscent of Bananas Foster, these caramelized plantains are outrageously delicious!

INGREDIENTS

1 tablespoon butter

2 sweet plantains

1 teaspoon ground cinnamon

1 teaspoon freshly grated nutmeg

½ teaspoon sea salt

1 tablespoon sugar

⅓ cup apple juice

1 In a medium saucepan, melt the butter over medium heat. When butter is melted, add the salt and sugar to the pan. Cook until the sugar has dissolved and the mixture turns golden.

2 Peel and cut the plantains into slices that are ⅓-inch thick. Toss them into the saucepan and cook until tender, approximately four minutes.

3 Pour the apple juice into the pan and bring to a boil. Cook until sauce has thickened, approximately one minute. Remove pan from the heat and stir in the cinnamon and nutmeg.

4 Scoop into serving dishes. Top each dish with some of the extra juice, and garnish with ice cream or whipped cream.

Grilled Peaches with Pistachios

**MAKES 4-8 SERVINGS • ACTIVE TIME: 15 MINUTES
TOTAL TIME: 15 MINUTES**

Grilling the peaches adds a caramelized boost that you can't get from the oven. Enjoy these year-round!

1 Cut the peaches in half and remove the pits.

2 Place the butter in a small saucepan and cook until melted. Stir in cardamom and salt. Remove from heat.

3 Brush each half-peach with the butter. Make sure to brush both sides.

4 Heat grill to 350° F and then place the peaches on the grill. Cook for 3-4 minutes on each side.

5 When serving, top with a scoop of vanilla ice cream and a sprinkle of chopped pistachios.

INGREDIENTS

4 ripe peaches

2 tablespoons butter

2 tablespoons honey

¼ teaspoon ground cardamom

¼ teaspoon sea salt

Chopped pistachios for garnish

Light Strawberry-Blueberry Trifle

MAKES 8-10 SERVINGS • ACTIVE TIME: 20 MINUTES
TOTAL TIME: 20 MINUTES

This trifle is airy and light, making it perfect for any party. It's also a great way to make the most of your summer fruit!

INGREDIENTS

1 angel food cake

1 lb. fresh strawberries

1 lb. fresh blueberries

¼ cup water

2 tablespoons granulated sugar

2 tablespoons freshly squeezed lemon juice

2 8-oz. packages of cream cheese

1 cup powdered sugar

2 cups heavy whipping cream

1 teaspoon pure vanilla extract

¼ teaspoon sea salt

1 Place water, granulated sugar, and lemon juice in saucepan and cook until sugar dissolves. Remove pan from heat and let cool.

2 Slice the strawberries.

3 Place the cream cheese and powdered sugar in the bowl of an electric mixer and until light and fluffy. Slowly add the heavy cream to the bowl and whisk until well combined. You want the contents of the bowl to look like whipped cream. Add the vanilla extract and salt, and mix until combined.

4 Slice the angel food cake and place the slices in a layer at the bottom of a trifle dish. Pour roughly ⅓ of the lemon simple syrup over the cake. Spread approximately ⅓ of the cream on top of this. Place half of the strawberry slices on top of the cream. Top with layers of cake, syrup, and cream. Sprinkle half of the blueberries onto the cream. Top blueberries with cake, syrup, and cream. Then decorate the top with the remaining fruit and serve!

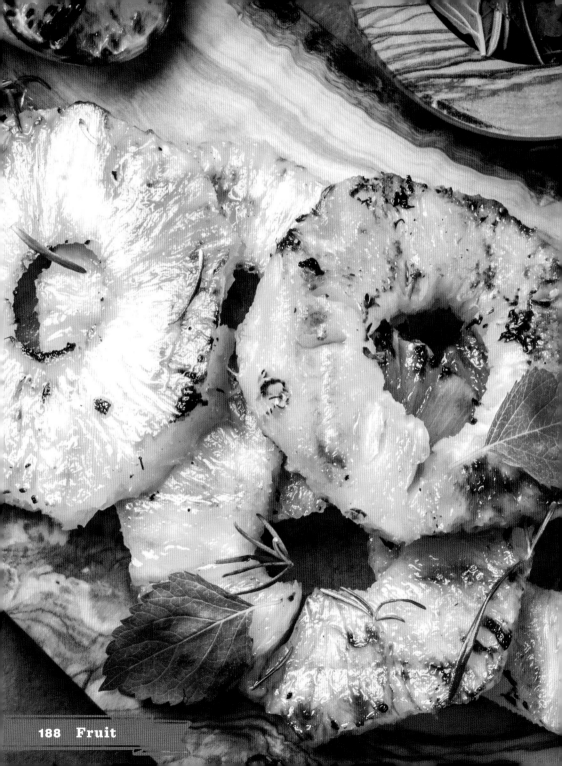

Grilled Pineapple

**MAKES 4-6 SERVINGS • ACTIVE TIME: 15 MINUTES
TOTAL TIME: 15 MINUTES**

Sweet and smoky pineapple is the perfect partner for vanilla ice cream or maple whipped cream.

1 Place pineapple rings on a baking sheet.

2 Combine the butter, sugar, salt, and spices in a bowl.

3 Brush all sides of the pineapple with the butter.

4 Heat grill to 350° F. Place pineapples onto the hot grill and cook for 8-10 minutes, turning once or twice and brushing with any extra butter. The pineapple is ready when it has turned golden brown. Remove from grill and serve.

INGREDIENTS

1 fresh pineapple, peeled and cut into rings

½ cup butter, melted

½ cup brown sugar

½ teaspoon sea salt

1 teaspoon ground cinnamon

½ teaspoon freshly grated nutmeg

¼ teaspoon ground cardamom

Candies & Confections

Take it from me: Homemade candies and confections are life changing. My experiences started with my aunt, who had me help her make homemade salted caramels and homemade marshmallows. I couldn't believe how easy they were to make, how much fun I had, and how delicious they ended up being. And, obviously, I wouldn't be writing this book if those times hadn't made a big impression on me.

While caramels and marshmallows are far from difficult to make, there are a number of recipes that are even easier. If you find yourself unsure where to start or low on time, give the chocolate candies or the white chocolate bark a try—you'll end up with a delightful treat that still looks impressive. Since these candies make for perfect party favors and great gifts around the holidays, they'll also get you on everyone's good side. In fact, the only issue you'll have is convincing everyone that they're homemade!

Peanut Butter Cups

MAKES 12 CUPS • ACTIVE TIME: 15 MINUTES
TOTAL TIME: 1 HOUR AND 15 MINUTES

These are the real deal—even better than store-bought!

INGREDIENTS

- 1 cup creamy peanut butter
- ½ cup powdered sugar
- ½ teaspoon sea salt
- ¼ teaspoon pure vanilla extract
- 12 oz. semi-sweet chocolate chips

1 Combine the peanut butter, sugar, salt, and vanilla in a bowl. If you need to soften the peanut butter, microwave for 15-30 seconds.

2 Place chocolate chips in microwave-safe bowl and then microwave for $1\frac{1}{2}$-2 minutes, removing once or twice to stir.

3 Place muffin liners in muffin tin and lightly grease the liners.

4 Place a spoonful of chocolate in each muffin liner and then use spoon to drag chocolate $\frac{1}{3}$-$\frac{1}{2}$ of the way up the sides. When you have done this for each liner, place in refrigerator and let chill for 15-20 minutes, until chocolate has hardened.

5 Remove from refrigerator, scoop peanut butter into each hardened chocolate shell and smooth out. Return to refrigerator and chill for 10-15 minutes.

6 Remove from refrigerator, top each cup with another spoonful of melted chocolate, and smooth. Return to refrigerator and chill for 25-30 minutes before serving.

Homemade No-Cook Fudge

MAKES 25-35 PIECES • ACTIVE TIME: 5 MINUTES
TOTAL TIME: 5 MINUTES

My grandfather used to make this every Christmas! It's easy, fun, and delicious.

1 Place milk and chocolate chips in a microwave-safe bowl and microwave for 30 seconds.

2 Remove from microwave and let sit for one minute. Stir until smooth. If necessary, return to microwave.

3 Add vanilla, salt, and marshmallows, if you are using them. Stir until thoroughly combined. Line baking dish with lightly buttered parchment paper. Pour mixture into baking dish and allow to cool for 40-50 minutes before serving.

INGREDIENTS

1 can sweetened condensed milk

12 oz. semi-sweet chocolate chips

1 teaspoon pure vanilla extract

½ teaspoon sea salt

1 cup mini-marshmallows (optional)

Rice Crispies Treats

MAKES 15-20 SERVINGS • ACTIVE TIME: 10 MINUTES
TOTAL TIME: 40 MINUTES

One of the most classic desserts of all time. They never fail to please!

INGREDIENTS

8 cups crispy rice cereal

1 bag regular marshmallows

1 bag mini-marshmallows

5 tablespoons butter

½ teaspoon pure vanilla extract

½ teaspoon sea salt

1 Place butter in a large saucepan and cook over medium heat until it is melted. Add regular and mini-marshmallows and stir often, until marshmallows are also melted.

2 Add vanilla and salt and stir until combined. Add the cereal and stir gently, making sure the marshmallow coats the cereal evenly.

3 Remove saucepan from heat. Grease a nine-by-thirteen-inch baking dish and pour the contents of the saucepan into it. Grease your hands with a little vegetable oil or butter and press the mixture into an even layer. Allow to rest for 30 minutes before cutting into desired shapes and serving.

Oreo Crispies Treats

**MAKES 8-10 SERVINGS • ACTIVE TIME: 10 MINUTES
TOTAL TIME: 40 MINUTES**

A fun take on the classic rice crispies treat.

INGREDIENTS

1 package regular Oreos

1 bag regular marshmallows

1 bag mini-marshmallows

4 tablespoons butter

¼ teaspoon sea salt

1 Place butter in large saucepan and cook over medium heat until butter is melted. Add regular and mini-marshmallows and stir often, until marshmallows are also melted.

2 Place cookies in a large gallon bag and crush until they are small but not too fine.

3 Add cookie pieces to saucepan and stir until the cookies are evenly coated. Remove saucepan from heat.

4 Remove saucepan from heat. Grease a nine-by-thirteen-inch baking dish and pour the contents of the saucepan into it. Grease your hands with a little vegetable oil or butter and press the mixture into an even layer. Let rest for 20-30 minutes before cutting into desired shapes and serving.

Cookies-and-Cream Bark

MAKES 10-12 SERVINGS • ACTIVE TIME: 15 MINUTES
TOTAL TIME: 1 HOUR AND 15 MINUTES

I love cutting this bark into little bars for parties. It is also great to keep in the freezer for a little mid-week treat.

INGREDIENTS

2 12-oz. bags white chocolate chips

1 package regular Oreos

1 Bring ½ inch of water to boil in a saucepan. Add white chocolate chips to a bowl and place bowl over the saucepan. Cook until chocolate is melted and then remove bowl from heat.

2 Line baking sheet with a lightly greased piece of parchment paper. Pour chocolate onto sheet.

3 Place Oreos in a large plastic bag and crush into bite-size pieces.

4 Top white chocolate with crushed Oreos. Place baking sheet in refrigerator or freezer for a minimum of one hour. Break into large chunks before serving.

Marshmallows

You will be amazed by how fun it is to make homemade marshmallows.

INGREDIENTS

1 cup water

3 packages of unflavored gelatin

1 ½ cups sugar

1 cup light corn syrup

2 teaspoons pure vanilla extract

½ teaspoon sea salt

1 Place ½ cup of the water in the bowl of a standing mixer. Sprinkle the gelatin into the water and let it dissolve.

2 Place remaining water, sugar, and corn syrup in a medium saucepan. Cook over medium heat and swirl the pan a few times, until the mixture begins to bubble. You want the mixture to reach about 240° F on a candy thermometer. When this temperature is reached, remove saucepan from heat and let stand for one minute.

3 Run the whisk attachment on the standing mixer while slowly pouring the contents of the saucepan down the side of the mixing bowl. Gradually increase the speed of the mixer until the mixture is white, fluffy and glossy. Add the vanilla.

4 Lightly grease a nine-inch baking dish and sprinkle powdered sugar through a sieve until the dish is completely coated. Pour marshmallow mixture into baking dish and use a greased or wet spatula to even out the top of the marshmallow. Let marshmallows cool for at least five hours.

5 When ready to serve, dust cutting surface, knife, and hands with powdered sugar to prevent sticking. Cut marshmallows into cubes and serve!

Variations: Add whatever flavor or color you desire. Examples: almond extract, lemon extract, cocoa powder, any color food coloring, etc.

Nougat

It took me a while to come around on nougat, but as soon as I did, I thought it imperative that I learn to make it!

INGREDIENTS

3 large egg whites

1 cup sugar

½ cup light corn syrup

¼ cup water

1 tablespoon pure vanilla extract

¾ teaspoon sea salt

1 Use an electric mixer to whip egg whites until they are frothy.

2 Add sugar, corn syrup, and water to saucepan and bring to a boil. Cook until candy thermometer reads 240° F.

3 Add a splash of the hot syrup to the egg whites while the mixer is running on low. Once combined, gently pour the rest of the syrup into the egg whites with the mixer continuing to run. Gradually increase the speed and mix until light and frothy. Add the vanilla and salt and continue mixing until stiff peaks begin to form. Let cool. Serve plain or use in candy bars.

Sweet Potato Candies

**MAKES 20 CANDIES • ACTIVE TIME: 45 MINUTES
TOTAL TIME: 2-4 HOURS**

I love to serve these in the fall when the air is getting crisp and the leaves are as orange as the potatoes. You can flavor these little candies any way you like. So versatile!

INGREDIENTS

1 lb. sweet potatoes

2 cups sugar

¼ cup honey

1 cup water

Zest of 1 lime

¼ cup freshly squeezed lime juice

½ teaspoon sea salt

¼ teaspoon freshly ground nutmeg

Powdered sugar for dusting

1 To cook the sweet potatoes, poke a few holes in them with a fork. Microwave on high for 8-10 minutes, or until the inside is tender when poked with a fork. You may want to flip the potato once or twice as it cooks. When sweet potatoes are cooked, let stand until they are cool enough to handle.

2 Scoop out the insides of the potatoes and run them through a food mill. Add the honey, lime zest, lime juice, salt, and nutmeg and stir until combined.

3 Place sugar and water in a saucepan and warm over medium heat until a candy thermometer reads approximately 255° F. Remove from heat and let stand for one minute.

4 Gently stir the sweet potato mixture into the pan containing the syrup. Once combined, cook over medium heat until the mixture is thick enough that you can run a spoon through it and leave a canal. Remove from heat. Line a baking sheet with wax paper. Pour contents of pan onto baking sheet so that it rests evenly. Let cool.

5 Once cooled completely, start cutting the candy into little pieces. I've found that Tootsie Roll-sized pieces are best, but whatever size and shape you prefer is fine. Before cutting, dust knife, your hands, and cutting surface with powdered sugar to prevent sticking.

6 Wrap each candy in a little piece of parchment paper and twist both ends in opposite directions to seal.

Variations: Spices like cinnamon, allspice, cayenne pepper, cardamom, or shredded coconut are fun twists on this dessert.

Mexican Hot Chocolate

MAKES 4-5 SERVINGS • ACTIVE TIME: 15 MINUTES
TOTAL TIME: 15 MINUTES

This hot chocolate is so lush and flavorful that you don't need to eat anything else with it! The perfect beverage while sitting by the fire on a cold night.

1 Place milk, half-and-half, cinnamon sticks, and chili pepper in a saucepan and cook over medium-low heat for 5-6 minutes, making sure mixture does not boil. Remove cinnamon sticks and chili pepper.

2 Once mixture is hot, add the sweetened condensed milk and whisk until combined. Add the chocolate and cook until chocolate is melted, stirring occasionally. Add the vanilla, nutmeg, and salt and whisk until combined. Taste the hot chocolate and season to your preference. Ladle into mugs and top with whipped cream.

INGREDIENTS

3 cups whole milk

1 cup half-and-half

¼ cup sweetened condensed milk

2 bags semi-sweet chocolate chips

3 cinnamon sticks

½ teaspoon pure vanilla extract

1 dried red chili pepper

1 teaspoon freshly grated nutmeg

½ teaspoon sea salt

Pumpkin Spice Latte

**MAKES 1 LARGE OR 2 SMALL LATTES • ACTIVE TIME: 5-10 MINUTES
TOTAL TIME: 5-10 MINUTES**

For the pumpkin lovers out there, this hot drink is perfect for dessert—or if you want to spice up your usual coffee.

INGREDIENTS

¾ **cup whole milk**

¼ **cup brewed espresso**

1 **tablespoon pumpkin puree**

⅛ **teaspoon ground cinnamon**

⅛ **teaspoon freshly grated nutmeg**

⅛ **teaspoon allspice**

1 **teaspoon light brown sugar**

1 In a saucepan, combine milk, pumpkin, spices, and brown sugar and cook over medium-low heat until hot but not boiling. Make sure everything is dissolved.

2 Remove from heat and whisk milk until it is frothy.

3 Brew espresso and pour frothy milk over it. Top with a sprinkle of cinnamon and enjoy!

Candied Apples

Would it really be autumn without candied apples? This is an easy way to use up all those apples you picked at the local orchard.

1 Place the sugar, corn syrup, and water in a medium saucepan and cook over high heat, swirling a few times. When the syrup begins to boil, lower the heat to medium-high and continue to boil for approximately 20 minutes, until a candy thermometer reads just over 300° F. Remove from heat. Stir in food coloring.

2 Insert popsicle sticks into apples and dip them in the syrup, turning to ensure they are completely coated. Set candy-coated apples on a lightly greased baking sheet and let stand until candy shell is hard.

INGREDIENTS

2 cups sugar

½ cup light corn syrup

¾ cup water

4 apples

2-3 drops red food coloring

Homemade Candy Bar (100 Grand)

MAKE 20 CANDIES (DEPENDING ON SIZE) • ACTIVE TIME: 15 MINUTES
TOTAL TIME: 1 HOUR AND 30 MINUTES

Homemade candy is always the way to go. With this recipe, there's no need to wait until Halloween!

INGREDIENTS

1 block soft caramel, or 1 bag soft caramel squares

1 lb. semi-sweet chocolate

1½ cups Rice Krispies cereal

1 If using a block of caramel, cut into 1-inch slices. Place caramels in refrigerator until firm.

2 Boil ½ inch of water in saucepan. Place chocolate in a bowl and put bowl over saucepan. When chocolate is melted and smooth, add Rice Krispies and mix until cereal is coated.

3 Dip the caramels into the chocolate mixture and place on a baking sheet lined with wax paper. Place in refrigerator and chill for at least one hour before serving.

Candied Citrus Peels

**MAKES 30 CANDIED PEELS • ACTIVE TIME: 1 HOUR AND 10 MINUTES
TOTAL TIME: 1 HOUR AND 40 MINUTES**

The first time I had a candied orange peel was at an NYC restaurant atop an unforgettable bowl of hot chocolate. These little candies are great to have on hand—whether it be for snacking or an impressive garnish.

INGREDIENTS

4 large oranges

4 cups sugar

4 cups water

1 Cut the top and bottom off of each orange. Very gently remove the skin from the fruit, trying to keep it in one piece or at most a few large pieces. Once the skin has been removed, remove any extra white pith from the inside of the zest, since it tends to be bitter. Take the orange ring and cut into approximately ¼-inch strips.

2 Place strips in a medium saucepan and cover with water. Bring to boil and cook for two minutes. Drain and cover peels with cold water again. Bring to a boil and cook for two more minutes. Remove from heat, drain, and remove strips from pan.

3 Place the sugar and water in the saucepan and bring to a boil. Cook until sugar is completely dissolved. Add the orange strips to the boiling syrup and reduce heat to medium-low. Simmer for about one hour, then remove from heat and let the strips cool in the syrup.

4 Remove the strips from the syrup and pat dry. Roll them in sugar and let stand for 30 minutes. Serve on top of ice cream, hot chocolate, in fruit salad, or enjoy like a piece of candy!

Variations: Use lime, lemon, grapefruit, or blood orange peels!

Candied Pumpkin Seeds

MAKES 1 CUP • ACTIVE TIME: 15 MINUTES
TOTAL TIME: 45 MINUTES – 1 HOUR

Sprinkle these sweet seeds on top of pumpkin cheesecake or gingersnap ice cream. They add the perfect crunch to all kinds of desserts.

1 Place butter in saucepan and melt over medium heat. Add sugar, honey, all of the spices, and the salt. Stir until mixture is well-combined and sugar has dissolved. Add pumpkin seeds and cook until they are puffy and golden.

2 Remove saucepan from heat. Line baking sheet with parchment paper, pour seeds onto baking sheet and let cool completely. Once cool, break up any large pieces and serve over ice cream, cheesecake, or in fruit salad.

INGREDIENTS

1 cup pepitas (raw pumpkin seeds)

2 tablespoons butter

2 tablespoons sugar

1 teaspoon honey

½ teaspoon cinnamon

½ teaspoon ground allspice

½ teaspoon freshly grated nutmeg

½ teaspoon sea salt

Candied Mint, Sage or Basil

MAKES 12 LEAVES • ACTIVE TIME: 15 MINUTES
TOTAL TIME: 24 HOURS

Already love fresh herbs? Try using these candied versions on your favorite desserts. They are perfect for the holiday season.

INGREDIENTS

1 egg white, beaten (2 tablespoons corn syrup for vegan alternative)

½ cup sugar

1 tablespoon water

12 fresh mint leaves

1 Gently wash and dry the mint leaves.

2 Place egg white and water in a bowl and whisk until mixture is a little bit frothy.

3 Dip each mint leaf into the egg white and shake off the excess. Make sure to handle the leaves very delicately in order to avoid bruising.

4 Dip both sides of the leaf in the sugar. Line a baking sheet with parchment paper and lay leaves flat on the sheet. Let stand for 24 hours before serving.

Variations: Use rose petals, rosemary, thyme, or fresh ginger .

Salted Caramel Coconut Macaroons

MAKES 16-20 MACAROONS • ACTIVE TIME: 30 MINUTES
TOTAL TIME: 2 HOURS AND 15 MINUTES

Salted-caramel anything always catches my eye. Combine that with a chewy coconut macaroon and it is a true winner in my book!

1 Place the butter, milk, caramels, and salt in a small saucepan and cook over medium heat. Once the caramels and butter have melted, add the coconut and mix until the caramel is coated with coconut.

2 Line a baking sheet with parchment paper and scoop tablespoons of the caramel mixture from the saucepan. Place on baking sheet and let cool for one hour.

3 Place chocolate in a microwave-safe bowl and microwave on high until chocolate is melted, 15-30 seconds. Be careful not to overcook.

4 Dip the bottom of the cooled macaroons into the melted chocolate and place them back on the baking sheet. Once all the macaroons have been dipped, use the rest of the chocolate to drizzle over the top.

5 Place in refrigerator for 30-45 minutes before serving.

INGREDIENTS

6 tablespoons butter, melted

3 tablespoons milk

1 bag of soft caramels

4 cups shredded sweetened coconut

4 oz. dark chocolate, melted

1 teaspoon sea salt

Coconut Macaroons

MAKES 15-20 MACAROONS • ACTIVE TIME: 10 MINUTES
TOTAL TIME: 40 MINUTES

A perfect little bite that is both sweet and chewy. I love to dip these cookies in chocolate.

INGREDIENTS

1 cup shredded, unsweetened coconut

2 tablespoons honey

2 tablespoons coconut oil

½ cup all-purpose flour

1 teaspoon pure vanilla extract

¼ teaspoon sea salt

1 Combine all ingredients in a food processor and process until well combined.

2 Use spoon to scoop out one tablespoon-sized balls of the mixture. Roll into spheres. Line a baking sheet with parchment paper and place balls onto sheet. Refrigerate for 30 minutes before serving. For added taste and aesthetics, dip macaroons into melted chocolate!

Chocolate-Covered Graham Crackers

MAKES 4-6 SERVINGS • ACTIVE TIME: 10-15 MINUTES
TOTAL TIME: 1 HOUR AND 15 MINUTES

If you really want a treat, try dipping these in the Marshmallow Fluff Dip—indoor s'mores!

INGREDIENTS

10 graham crackers, broken into fourths

2 cups semi-sweet chocolate chips

1 tablespoon butter

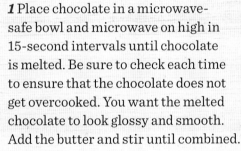

1 Place chocolate in a microwave-safe bowl and microwave on high in 15-second intervals until chocolate is melted. Be sure to check each time to ensure that the chocolate does not get overcooked. You want the melted chocolate to look glossy and smooth. Add the butter and stir until combined.

2 Dip half of the graham cracker into the chocolate. Line a baking sheet with wax paper and place coated graham crackers onto sheet. Once all of the graham crackers have been used, place the baking sheet in the refrigerator for a minimum of an hour, or until the chocolate is set.

Variation: Use 20 ginger snaps in place of the graham crackers.

Cookie Dough Pops

MAKES 15-20 POPS • ACTIVE TIME: 15 MINUTES
TOTAL TIME: 2-3 HOURS

These are a fun way to enjoy cookie dough without having to worry about raw egg! Great for birthday parties and summer BBQs.

1 Place the butter, sugar, and brown sugar in the bowl of an electric mixer and mix until it is light and fluffy. Add the salt and vanilla and mix until combined. Add the flour in two batches and continue to mix. Before flour is completely blended in, add the chocolate chips and mix until well combined. Cover directly with plastic wrap and place in refrigerator for one hour.

2 Line a baking sheet with parchment paper. Remove mixture from refrigerator and scoop out teaspoon-sized balls of dough. Roll into spheres and place on baking sheet. Stick toothpicks or little lollipop sticks into each sphere. If desired, melt ½ cup semi-sweet chocolate chips in the microwave on high for 15-20 seconds, or until smooth. Dip each pop into the melted chocolate and place them back on baking sheet. Let chill in refrigerator for 1-2 hours and then serve!

INGREDIENTS

1 stick butter, softened

⅓ cup granulated sugar

⅓ cup dark brown sugar

½ teaspoon sea salt

½ teaspoon pure vanilla extract

1 cup all-purpose flour

1 cup miniature semi-sweet chocolate chips

Chocolate Candies

These chocolate candies allow your creativity to shine! Try any kind of topping you want, make them all the same or make each one unique—the options are endless.

1 Place chocolate in a microwave-safe bowl and microwave on high for 25-30 seconds. Remove and stir until smooth. If necessary, return chocolate to microwave for a few more seconds.

2 Line a baking sheet with parchment paper. Scoop teaspoon-sized balls of the chocolate onto baking sheet. Spread the chocolate into flat disks and place desired toppings on the chocolates. Place in refrigerator for 30 minutes, or until chocolates are set.

INGREDIENTS

8 oz. bittersweet chocolate, melted

Dried cherries

Roasted almonds

Pistachios

Candied orange peels

Toasted pepitas

Fleur de sel (sea salt flakes)

White Chocolate Bark

MAKES 6-8 SERVINGS • ACTIVE TIME: 10 MINUTES
TOTAL TIME: 10 MINUTES

This is a great addition to any dessert table. You can also wrap up this bark for beautiful gifts.

INGREDIENTS

16 oz. white chocolate, chopped

½ cup dried cherries

½ cup shelled pistachios

½ cup dried apricots, chopped

1 Place ¾ of the chocolate in a microwave-safe bowl and microwave on high for approximately 40 seconds. Stir and return to microwave for 30 seconds. Add the remaining chocolate and stir until completely smooth.

2 Line baking sheet with parchment paper. Pour melted chocolate onto baking sheet and spread it into an even layer, making sure not to spread it too thin.

3 Sprinkle toppings onto the chocolate and lightly press down to ensure that they stick. Place in refrigerator for a minimum of 30 minutes.

4 When the chocolate is set, break the bark up into large pieces and serve!

Nutella Rice Crispies Bars

MAKES 12-24 SERVINGS (DEPENDS ON PREFERRED SIZE)
ACTIVE TIME: 10 MINUTES • TOTAL TIME: 30 MINUTES

Try using the homemade chocolate hazelnut spread (see recipe on page 251) in this recipe!

1 Place the butter in a large pot and cook until melted. Add the marshmallows and salt, and cook until the marshmallows are melted. Stir in the Nutella and mix until combined. Add the crispy rice cereal in two batches and stir until they are coated by the marshmallow/Nutella mixture.

2 Lightly butter a baking dish. Pour the coated cereal into the dish and press the mixture into an even layer. You will want to butter your hands before pressing. Let stand for at least 20 minutes before cutting into bars.

INGREDIENTS

2 sticks butter

2 bags mini-marshmallows

1 teaspoon sea salt

2 cups Nutella

12 cups crispy rice cereal

Sea salt, optional

Dips, Sauces, & Syrups

Never underestimate the power of a simple dip, sauce, or syrup. I love a dessert dip for the ease of transporting and the ease of sharing! And they're versatile, since many dips can double as spreads. A piece of advice: Don't be bashful about spreading these far and wide. I love using the chocolate hazelnut dip on a grilled cheese or atop toasted pound cake. Yes, I know the grilled cheese-and-chocolate combo sounds weird. But trust me, it's out of this world!

The syrup and sauce recipes that follow are great options if time isn't on your side. Pour them into ice cream sodas or drizzle over some shaved ice to make delicious snow cones. And don't be quick to dismiss them as mere toppings—they can take your dessert making to the next level. For instance, I steep fresh herbs or whole spices (cinnamon sticks, whole cloves, star anise, etc.) in some of these syrups to add depth and complexity to other desserts.

Cherry Snow Cone Syrup

MAKES ½ CUP - ¾ CUP OF SYRUP • ACTIVE TIME: 10 MINUTES
TOTAL TIME: 1 HOUR AND 10 MINUTES

When you forget to prepare a dessert, snow cones are a quick, easy, and inexpensive option to impress friends and family. All you need is to do is whip up this simple syrup and crush some ice! The easiest way to make crushed ice is to put ice into a blender. This recipe is also a great way to use up fruit that is a day or two past its prime.

INGREDIENTS

1 cup pitted cherries, fresh or frozen

¾ cup sugar

1 cup water

1 Place all ingredients into a saucepan and cook over medium-high heat.

2 Once the sugar has dissolved, mash the cherries to release their flavor and color. Cook until the contents of pan are syrupy.

3 Remove pan from heat and cool. When syrup has cooled, strain contents of pan into desired container.

4 Store container in refrigerator until ready to serve over ice.

Variations: Lemon: Zest of one lemon, one cup fresh lemon juice, one cup sugar; Orange: Zest of one orange, one cup fresh orange juice, one cup sugar; Blueberry: three cups fresh or frozen blueberries, $3/4$ cup water, $1/4$ cup sugar, juice of $1/2$ a lemon; Apple: two cups apple juice, $1/4$ cup sugar, one cinnamon stick (optional, if you want a hint of spice); Peach: one cup fresh or frozen peaches, one cup sugar, $1/2$ cup water; Watermelon: four cups puréed watermelon, $3/4$ cup sugar

Chocolate Syrup

for Ice Cream Sodas

**MAKES 1 CUP OF SYRUP • ACTIVE TIME: 10 MINUTES
TOTAL TIME: 10 MINUTES**

Chocolate syrup is a staple in my fridge. Drizzle it on anything and everything.

1 Combine cocoa powder, water, sea salt, sugar, and coffee grounds in a saucepan. Cook over medium heat until sugar has been dissolved, approximately 5-6 minutes.

2 Remove from heat. Add the vanilla to saucepan, stir, and let mixture cool.

3 Pour syrup into container and refrigerate. It is perfect for ice cream sodas, and also lovely as a topping in a bowl of ice cream.

INGREDIENTS

1 cup unsweetened cocoa powder

1¼ cup water

½ teaspoon sea salt

1⅔ cup sugar

¾ teaspoon instant coffee grounds

1½ teaspoons pure vanilla extract

Raspberry Syrup

for Ice Cream Sodas

MAKES 1 CUP • ACTIVE TIME: 2 MINUTES
TOTAL TIME: 4 HOURS

Any fizzy drink will enjoy the sweetness this syrup adds!

INGREDIENTS

1 pint fresh
raspberries

¼ cup freshly
squeezed lemon juice

½ cup sugar

1 tablespoon honey

1 Combine all ingredients in a bowl, cover, and place into refrigerator. Chill for a minimum of four hours, until raspberries have started to break down and release their liquid. For best results, chill overnight.

2 Remove mixture from refrigerator and pour through a fine sieve. Use your hands to push liquid through the sieve.

3 Pour syrup into a container and store in refrigerator until ready to use.

4 Variation: Strawberries, blueberries, peaches, and blackberries are all wonderful options. And don't be cautious—this syrup is so good that almost any fruit can be used!

Cool Whip

Get your strawberries ready!

1 Combine gelatin and water in a small saucepan. Simmer until gelatin is completely dissolved.

2 Place heavy cream in a bowl and whisk until it begins to thicken. Add sugar and gelatin. Add remaining ingredients and whisk until stiff peaks begin to form.

3 Place in refrigerator until ready to serve.

INGREDIENTS

2 teaspoons unflavored gelatin

½ cup water

2 ⅓ cup heavy cream

1 cup powdered sugar

2 teaspoons pure vanilla extract

Whipped Cream

MAKES 2 CUPS • ACTIVE TIME: 5-7 MINUTES
TOTAL TIME: 5-7 MINUTES

Use this recipe to top pie, pound cake, ice cream, fresh fruit, anything. Don't be intimidated—whipped cream is incredibly easy to "whip up."

INGREDIENTS

2 cups heavy whipping cream

1 teaspoon pure vanilla extract

1 Place cream and vanilla extract in bowl and whisk until soft peaks begin to form. Be sure not to over-mix, as this will result in butter.

2 Place in refrigerator until ready to serve.

Variation: Add one teaspoon cinnamon, one tablespoon pure maple syrup, or $1/2$ teaspoon cardamom.

Chocolate Hazelnut Dip

MAKES 1-1 ½ CUPS • ACTIVE TIME: 15-20 MINUTES
TOTAL TIME: 20-30 MINUTES

Also known as Nutella, this homemade version is 100 times more flavorful and enchanting.

1 Place hazelnuts in a dry skillet and cook over medium heat until fragrant, approximately one minute. Be sure not to burn the hazelnuts. Remove hazelnuts from pan and allow to cool. When hazelnuts are cool, place in food processor with sugar and salt. Blend until a paste forms.

2 Boil ½ inch water in saucepan. Place chocolate pieces into a bowl and set bowl on top of pan, forming a double boiler.

3 When chocolate is melted, remove from heat, add butter and cream, and whisk until combined. Add hazelnut paste and whisk until thoroughly combined.

4 Once combined, let chill. Serve with fresh fruit, on pound cake, or spread on a piece of toast for a delicious breakfast.

INGREDIENTS

2 cups hazelnuts

⅓ cup sugar

1 teaspoon sea salt

16 oz. semi-sweet chocolate, chopped

1 stick butter

1 cup heavy whipping cream

Creme Anglaise

MAKES 1 ½ CUPS • ACTIVE TIME: 20 MINUTES
TOTAL TIME: 20 MINUTES

Pour this over fresh fruit, cake, or ice cream to make dessert even more special!

INGREDIENTS

1 cup whole milk

1 cup heavy cream

¼ cup sugar

1 vanilla bean, seeds scraped out

4 large egg yolks

2 tablespoons spiced rum

1 Combine milk, cream, and rum in a medium saucepan. Scrape the seeds from the vanilla bean and add the seeds to saucepan. Cook over medium-high heat and bring mixture to a boil. Remove saucepan from heat.

2 Place sugar and egg yolks in a bowl and whisk until pale yellow. Add milk mixture to bowl before the saucepan's contents have cooled completely. Make sure to add milk mixture slowly while whisking constantly. When ingredients have been thoroughly combined, return mixture to saucepan.

3 Cook over low heat until the mixture thickens, approximately five minutes. Be careful not to boil.

4 Remove saucepan from heat and strain contents into bowl. Cover bowl and place in refrigerator until ready to serve.

S'mores Dip

Since no utensils are needed, this is perfect for a party. Just make sure you've got plenty of graham crackers.

1 Place cream cheese, $^2/_3$ cup of heavy cream and the Fluff in a bowl, and beat until fluffy. Fold in the mini-marshmallows and graham cracker crumbs.

2 Place pudding mix and remaining cream in a separate bowl, stir until combined and let stand.

3 Place a layer of the marshmallow mixture on the bottom of a serving bowl. Top with a layer of the pudding mixture. Alternate layers until you reach the top of the serving bowl. Try to have a layer of the marshmallow mixture at the top. Stick a knife long enough to reach the bottom of the bowl into the dip and swirl several times. Serve with graham crackers.

INGREDIENTS

8 oz. cream cheese

¾ cup powdered sugar

1 ½ cup Marshmallow Fluff

4 cups heavy whipping cream

1 package chocolate pudding

1 cup mini-marshmallows

¼ cup graham cracker crumbs

Marshmallow Fluff Dip

MAKES 1 ½ CUPS • ACTIVE TIME: 5 MINUTES
TOTAL TIME: 5 MINUTES

Dip chocolate-covered graham crackers in this cloud-like dip for a whimsical take on s'mores. If you have a kitchen torch, you can even caramelize the top of the dip for a dramatic effect.

INGREDIENTS

8 oz. Marshmallow Fluff

4 oz. cream cheese

1 cup powdered sugar

Mix all ingredients in a bowl. Serve with cookies or fruit.

Greek Yogurt Dip for Fruit Platter

MAKES 1 ½ CUPS • ACTIVE TIME: 5 MINUTES
TOTAL TIME: 5 MINUTES

Fresh fruit and this dip were made for each other. The nutmeg adds just a little "je ne sais quoi."

Place ingredients in a bowl and mix until well combined. Let chill. Serve with fruit.

INGREDIENTS

1 cup plain Greek yogurt

¼ cup honey

½ teaspoon freshly ground nutmeg

½ teaspoon sea salt

Maple Butter

MAKES 1 ½ CUPS • ACTIVE TIME: 5 MINUTES
TOTAL TIME: 5 MINUTES

Feel free to spread maple butter on hot waffles, pancakes, toast, and just about anything in the world.

INGREDIENTS

1 stick butter, softened

½ cup pure maple syrup

¼ teaspoon cinnamon

¼ teaspoon freshly grated nutmeg

1 Place butter into the bowl of an electric mixer and beat until light and fluffy. Add the cinnamon and nutmeg and mix until combined. While the mixer is running, slowly pour in the maple syrup and beat until the mixture is light. Make sure to scrape down the sides a few times.

2 Place the maple butter into a serving bowl. Serve immediately or place in refrigerator until ready to serve.

Hot Fudge

MAKES 2 CUPS • ACTIVE TIME: 15 MINUTES
TOTAL TIME: 15 MINUTES

As we all know, hot fudge is the perfect addition to any bowl of ice cream.

1 Place the cream, corn syrup, brown sugar, cocoa powder, salt, four ounces of the chocolate, and the espresso grounds in a medium saucepan and cook over medium heat.

2 When chocolate is melted, reduce heat and simmer for five minutes.

3 Remove from heat and whisk in the remaining chocolate, butter, and vanilla.

4 Serve over ice cream, cake, fresh fruit, anything—this delicious topping can do it all!

INGREDIENTS

⅔ cup heavy whipping cream

½ cup light corn syrup

⅓ cup dark brown sugar

¼ cup cocoa powder, unsweetened

½ teaspoon sea salt

8 oz. bittersweet chocolate, chopped

2 tablespoons butter

1 teaspoon pure vanilla extract

½ teaspoon instant espresso grounds

Cannoli Cream Dip

**MAKES 6-8 SERVINGS • ACTIVE TIME: 5 MINUTES
TOTAL TIME: 1 HOUR AND 5 MINUTES**

Enjoy this dip with pizzelle cookies or waffle cone pieces.

INGREDIENTS

8 oz. cream cheese

2 cups fresh
ricotta cheese

1½ cups
powdered sugar

1½ teaspoons
vanilla extract

¼ teaspoon sea salt

1 cup miniature
semi-sweet
chocolate chips

1 Place the cream cheese, ricotta, powdered sugar, salt, and vanilla in a bowl and beat until light and fluffy.

2 Fold in the chocolate chips and place in refrigerator for a minimum of one hour before serving.

Index

ABOUT THE AUTHOR

Mamie Fennimore is a Philadelphia native living and working as a writer and wine seller in Manhattan's Upper East Side. Mamie is a certified sommelier and former cheesemonger for two of NYC's most reputable cheese companies, and loves to share her knowledge through teaching wine and cheese pairing courses. Her passion for food started at a young age and truly solidified after her time living in the south of France. It was the French lifestyle that inspired her to share the importance of quality ingredients and accompaniments for meals (especially desserts!) to bring loved ones to the table. Mamie is also the author of *Salsas and Dips* and *Dressings*.

ABOUT CIDER MILL PRESS BOOK PUBLISHERS

Good ideas ripen with time. From seed to harvest, Cider Mill Press brings fine reading, information, and entertainment together between the covers of its creatively crafted books. Our Cider Mill bears fruit twice a year, publishing a new crop of titles each spring and fall.

VISIT US ONLINE AT
cidermillpress.com

OR WRITE TO US AT
12 Spring Street
PO Box 454
Kennebunkport, Maine 04046